Biba was born in Kenya, the first-born in the family of seven, four girls and three boys. His grandfather moved the family from the top of Manga escarpment in the then Kisii highlands southwards to virgin land, where he curved out what was then considered huge tract but in fact a couple of hectares! Much later, when the colonial authorities presented him with a choice to host a school or church, without second thoughts, he chose the Seventh Day Adventist Church. "Unlike the school, the church grows beyond its borders without eating up your land," was his logic. From this humble origin, his eldest grandson obtained earlier education before venturing into schools in various parts of the country, and university, graduating in medicine before specialising in surgery and public health. He has worked for universities and governments in Eastern Africa, the horn of Africa and Southern Africa. He is married with four children.

To Archie, Brian, Michelle, Peter (Jr.) and generations to come.

Biba

HAKUNA MATATA

AUSTIN MACAULEY PUBLISHERS™

LONDON • CAMBRIDGE • NEW YORK • SHARJAH

A CIP catalogue record for this title is available from the British Library.

ISBN 9781528901048 (Paperback)
ISBN 9781528956963 (ePub e-book)

www.austinmacauley.com

First Published (2019)
Austin Macauley Publishers Ltd
25 Canada Square
Canary Wharf
London
E14 5LQ

This book is the product of collective experiences, nuances and dreams. Any attempt to name all those whose contributions I should acknowledge will not be fair. Therefore, suffice to state that without Akoko Orinda, Peter Nyagonchong'a, James Wambura, Eric Sing'ombe, Said Osman, and George Rae, this book would never have been possible. Many decades of dialogue, shared struggles and dreams; heated arguments, disagreements and reconciliatory conversation; not only provided to help shape ideas but more importantly the trajectory and substance of the book. The notion of this book, reflecting on real events and situations may not have led to this narrative without the prompting by Alberto Gallachi. His role as my mentor, as we shared one desk for many years; him as project manager and myself as 'permanent casual worker' as he categorised my employment was provocative and inspirational. Each moment with Charles Nyameino and Joseph Orina is a live but unwritten soap opera. Narrating some earlier experiences helped me crystallise the soul and spirit of this book. It is impossible to measure the contribution of Jacob Mufunda, Ghirmay Andemichael, Usman Abdulmuni, Andrew Kosia, Saleh Meki, Musi Khumalo, and the senior management of the UN team in Eritrea, who made life in the country bearable through endless stories and great sense of humour. The final text was only possible through the painstaking efforts by Christian Hunter and Colleta Kandemiri. Finally, the many friends who over the years helped to help me steer an even life course, we cannot finish thanking you. No doubt, every reader who derives pleasure from reading this book adds an ounce here and a pound there of much deserved gratitude.

A Book of Light Entertainment and Mild Wisdom

Life is more than being alive. It is being human. One is a human being, not a human creature. It is your relationship with others, the people who matter, the people who do not matter, the environment, the climate, or just the weather.

Today I am sitting here all alone. Silence surrounds me from all sides. I am like a male goose standing alone near a water pond for a female, always expecting a female companion to arrive but no avail. What do I feel? A happy hermit, or bamboozled like Saeri's watermill at the onset of the dry season?

I am a rudderless ship adrift in the ocean of life!

Salimo was watching the clouds float away in the sky as he sat turning these and many thoughts that were running through his mind like a broken dam. A floodgate in his mind had broken, tormenting him like never before.

Sitting under the only casuarina tree in the homestead, Salimo was exploring the inner depths of his dark mind. He was trying to detangle the cobwebs suffocating his life.

"When did the rains begin to drench my body, my soul and my entire being?" he wondered.

"What I need is to be in motion; to keep moving like the untamed westerly air currents from the tropical forests of Africa across the Atlantic, transporting moisture to distant lands!"

"I have to move or I lose myself. I have to escape my shadow. Motion is overcoming life's resultant forces of inertia."

Salimo O'Masaii had just returned from Mombasa where he visited many nightspots, especially one with a striking name – Casuarinas. Regina Akinyi had an expensive commodity – Michelle, an associate from Bordeaux in France, as it was popularly known.

Salimo O'Masaii wondered if one could take pre-exposure prophylaxis, what medics referred to as PEP, for protection against HIV infection.

As to be expected, he had twisted the health strategy from 'post-exposure' to 'pre-exposure', to suit his motivation.

"Michelle, do you know if there is any interaction between PEP and Viagra?" Salimo O'Masaii enquired of Michelle.

Michelle just laughed.

He lamented on how HIV had interfered with the enjoyment of life. It was not like the old times when Salimo O'Masaii was a medical student. This is when he dropped the Salimo part of his name and became known simply as Masaii.

It was during his medical school days that one John Odhiambo Opar, or simply "The Man of Letters" designed the "magic bullet" for the prevention of any sexually transmitted infection!

The Man of Letters recommended that, "one should swallow eight tetracycline capsules half an hour before actual sexual intercourse". However, he warned that "it had to be within the thirty-minute period or one risked serious infection". The concentration of the antibiotic peaked thirty minutes after ingestion and the concentration rapidly dropped to a non-prophylactic dose.

Secondly, he recommended that within 24 hours following a sexual 'encounter', as he called this transient relationship, one should take eight tablets of metronidazole, or Flagyll as it was commonly known.

Besides quinine tablets, metronidazole in the original formulation was probably one of the most nauseating medicinal chemicals. One would prefer avoiding wildcat sex than repeatedly enduring the torment of ingesting the substance. And of course for those who enjoyed their beer or TB (short for Tusker Baridi) as they called it, would avoid the stuff like a plague. The drug has a strong anti-abuse effect for alcohol lovers!

Of course one needed to take care of skin parasites such as body lice. This you achieved through a few sprays of an insecticide around the genitalia within twenty-four hours after sex!

10

The triple prevention notwithstanding, most medical students preferred to wait for any worrying symptoms and then injected themselves with one dose of some long-acting penicillin. Fortunately most sexually transmitted bacteria were susceptible to this wonder drug. Unknown then to the students was that Human Immunodeficiency Virus was lurking round the corner or that one could contract hepatitis infection through sex. Indeed, soon having sex was synonymous to "taking on risk".

The triple therapy, as the Man of Letters described this approach was not without risk in itself. There was at least one reported case of fatal poisoning from a too-generous spray of the popular insecticide. The victim was, however, not a medical student.

***

The year before had been scintillating! How did Masaii become so lonely?

From the very first day at the University, Masaii had made up his mind to enjoy every single day, and whenever opportunity presented itself, to make it spectacular.

"What is the point of doing anything if it does not make you happy or bring some tangible gains to you or to somebody that you know?" he often asked.

No wonder then, that on his first day at the department of biochemistry, when his professor asked Masaii why he wanted to study medicine, his answer was very simple and direct.

"Sir, so that I can become a doctor," Masaii found himself at the medical school not out of design but by swimming along the academic current. Those upstream were considered the "crème de la crème" and shunted to professional courses, leaving the rest at the mercy of the mighty river of fate: the force of its current, its twists and turns and finally the sea, wherein it discharged its contents.

Masaii was getting used to the reverence with which the village people held doctors. A rare species, he thought. Every time he informed inquisitive people about his future endeavour in medicine, they looked at him in awe. "A doctor is second to God," one elder added after heaping lavish congratulations on him.

The university to which Masaii was admitted was not exactly Oxford, Cambridge or Makerere. Nevertheless, for the calling to medicine, anywhere would do and he was going to make the best of it.

The students would soon have settled into the mundane pursuit of a medical career if one more of what was to become a recurrent upheaval at the university had not occurred. In its wisdom, the government had introduced fees for all university students. The government was reneging on its promise of free education and the students were not ready to accede to this. The decision had been shelved once before when Kenyatta's government sensed rebellion in its ranks. However, with the declining economy and the increasing numbers of students, there were no more options available to the regime. The ministry was ordered to implement the new policy without further delay.

And so on Masaii's second day at the medical school, the student leadership called for the boycott of classes and demonstrations.

The response from the state was swift and ruthless...

For the whole week the students engaged the police in running battles around the streets of Nairobi.

Many students were reported injured a result of "police brutality" as the student newsletter described the chaos.

"Police rioting on campus" was the headline on the front page of the Platform.

"The Commissioner of Police is your enemy number one," the newsletter called on the student body to unite as they had nothing to lose except "to break the chains of bondage". The student organisation was well organised with a President and Cabinet. It was authoritative with many connections, locally and internationally. All students were required to be members making annual contributions and electing its leaders. During this particular crisis, President had denounced the Vice Chancellor for playing golf at the Muthaiga Club while "burning issues remained unattended to".

By the end of the week, with no let-up in sight, the terse announcement came on the government radio station during its one o'clock news bulletin: "The university has been closed indefinitely due to student unrest, boycott of classes and destruction of property".

The University Council, on advice from the Senate, had ordered the university closed with immediate effect. The students were given until six o'clock to vacate the halls of residence.

This was to be the annual feature of the long road to becoming a doctor. During the five years at the medical school, there was one crisis after another, forcing students onto the streets. As the elite of society, they considered their duty to protect society from exploitation by the dictatorial regime. For the first time Masaii was surprised to learn that the medical students were no longer at the frontline of dissent or action. They were considered passive and conservative, "the fuel for the regime", as the student leader referred to them. It was also puzzling how few people in the society had sympathy with the students.

The dailies called them "spoiled brats who were ungrateful to the society that paid dearly for their education".

The numbers of students killed, injured or raped was always tucked in the inner pages of the dailies. The front page carried gruesome pictures of vandalised shops, charred tyres or bewildered motorists inspecting their cars with broken windscreens.

"Yours is a noble profession," the Vice Chancellor had declared in his welcome address to the medical students. He went on to advise them on how demanding the course was and that they would find twenty-four hours in a day too short for what they had to accomplish. He informed them that "fierce bees are a sign of prime honey", and therefore they should steadily work towards their goal. Masaii was not surprised at the end of the official period for switching courses that the class had shrunken by twenty to one hundred five. Indeed, student dropout was also to be an annual phenomenon, with only eighty-five students of the initial admission graduating.

With all students sent home, it was clear that not participating in riots did not absolve even the medical students from blame. It was during this boycott that the parliament was made to amend the constitution to make it an offence for anybody else to be referred to as, "President". Henceforth, the title "President" would be reserved for the Head of State.

Masaii spent the two-week university closure reflecting on whether he had made an error in choosing medicine over pharmacy. He had been admitted to a university in the United Kingdom to study pharmacy. He did not know what a pharmacist was or what role they played in the health of people beyond dispensing pills through a small window. He did not contemplate a lifetime of counting tablets.

Despite the exposition from the pharmacist at the Eros Chemist on what the course entailed and the bright future in manufacturing or research, Masaii could not foresee any glamour in this profession. "You would love pharmacognosy," she explained, hoping to recruit one disciple into her profession.

"I will think about it," were his last words on the subject.

He decided on medicine, well aware that he could always revert to pharmacy. The invitation letter had clearly stated that the offer of a place to study pharmacy was to last his entire lifetime. He could take it any time he wanted. And having so re-assured himself, Masaii immersed himself into his medical studies with a passion.

***

The first year at the medical school proved both exciting and disheartening. It was disheartening because of the calibre of teachers. Only much later did he realise that the universities in general were populated by untrained teachers. He could only single out a few professors who were best suited to the profession. For example, Galzigna, the professor of biochemistry who, though confined to a wheel chair, was most humorous and most polished in his approach to teaching.

It was Galzigna who recommended a periodic snooze during his lectures. His explanation was that, research had shown that concentration declined significantly after fifteen minutes of a lecture. Therefore, two to three minutes of sleep every fifteen minutes or so would replenish the brain with depleted energy and improve concentration. It was Professor Galzigna who introduced the open book examination at the school of medicine, much to the shock of the conservatives in the faculty.

Once when students reported a colleague who was referring to a textbook during the examination, he brushed it off casually. "As a doctor you will not be expected to know everything under the sun, but will be required to make reference to textbooks and scientific papers," he explained. "If the student knows what page to get the right answer from, then he is a good student," he concluded to the surprise of the class. Needless to say his was one of the most popular subjects.

Then there was Dr Fasana, the storyteller. His stories spanned all the seven continents and each of them suited the topic of his lecture.

"In China I was called to go and attend to a difficult delivery. After several hours of walking up and down the hills we finally arrived at the house of the mother in trouble," ran one such a story.

"I asked for the candle to be lit for me to be able to see and examine the woman. I then put my hand into the birth canal and delivered a healthy lad, who immediately sent a wave of happiness across the room. I then put my hand inside for the second time and out came another baby, a girl this time. To my surprise, as soon as I handed over the second twin, the father blew off the candle. When I asked him why he put off the light at the moment when we needed it most to deliver the placenta, he replied very politely, "it is the light which is attracting them." Evidently two babies were already too many and a third child would ruin the already impoverished family."

The topic for the lecture was on the Embryology of Twin Pregnancy.

While talking about causes of a retained placenta, Fasana started the lecture about an incident in the Congo where he was summoned to attend to a woman whose placenta wouldn't come out. He was shocked to find the woman lying on the ground with the cut placenta tied to the wall. When he enquired the reason for tying the placenta, he was told: "to prevent the placenta from retracting back into the womb."

It was Fasana who drew the attention to the class to the famous statement in the textbook of surgery by Bailey and Love; "never give the cup of new knowledge to the novice before the froth fully settles."

From Fasana and Galzigna, he learnt one more thing; that language was no barrier to communication for a good teacher. Both professors were barely fluent in English, yet their lectures were fully packed and external examiners rated the student performance very highly.

On the other end of the spectrum was the anatomy group except for Mr Walker and Joe. Joe was the founder of the school, also famed for transporting cadavers from about one thousand kilometres away on top of his Volkswagen Beetle. "This is how I built the medical school here in this country," he would proudly announce during the introductory lecture. Joe only gave one lecture to each successive class. The lecture was entitled "The Upright Posture of Man: the Role of the Gluteus Maximus". The gluteus muscles are the ones we sit on and when well formed in women are a source of much adulation and desire. According to Joe, these muscles have released the arms from the business of walking to that of 'reaching', hence the major difference between man and all other species. The only other evolutionary miracle in the view of the professor was the structure of the human thumb that enables man to perform complex manipulations with his fingers. The thumb allows one unique function; that of apposition of the fingers. With these assertions, Joe's lecture was finished and he was off to attend to other more inspirational matters of building the Medical School, which in his view was never-ending.

Professor Joe, in Masaii's view, was a saint who belonged together with Mother Teresa. It was left to Dr Walker to take the rest of the coursework from where Joe left it. He was a natural extension of Joe. The difference between the master and student was that Dr Walker had some other interests in comparative anatomy, thereby imposing on the students the need to learn the behaviour of velvet monkeys and how they plummeted from great heights and from tree to tree without encountering major disasters.

The first year was disheartening in more than one way. Firstly, the students never got proper preparation to transition from high school maggots imbibing knowledge from the teachers to independent learners that they were supposed to be on entering the university. For Masaii and his small group of friends, the university came with one more gift. This was the gift of freedom from one's parents and from controlling high school teachers. And so for the group it was time to make up for lost opportunities!

For the first half of the year, Masaii and his team lived as if they were on extended holidays where school was only what happened in class. As soon as the heavy yoke imposed in the lecture room fell off, learning stood adjourned until the next scheduled lecture. Their class work remained below average and nobody seemed to care until Tito Taabu got a wake-up call in form of a failed test.

"Gentlemen," Tito, or Otis as he was commonly called, sounded the alarm, "unless we change our ways, we will certainly fail."

Otis noted that Saturday and Sunday were definitely no-learning days. The Saturday bash commenced on Friday, the day that they enjoyed the long night of dancing, usually in the company of a newly-found female. This is the same person that you would spend the whole of Saturday with, including going to the shows and parting in the night. In preparation for Friday evening and a successful Saturday, the evening of Thursday was spent scouting for the relevant event taking place on Saturday and visiting various women's hostels in the city in search of suitable female company. Sunday was the day dedicated for the regular girlfriend. Tuesday evening, like Thursday, was spent nosing around for suitable company for the midweek dance at the Avenue Hotel, which at an all-time low cover charge of five shillings, entitled students to an extended night of having a nice time away from the horrible books. Surprisingly, it was only Monday evening that was available for serious reading.

"Gentlemen, with only one evening of studying do you think we will make it through this first year?" Otis asked the team.

It did not need any serious statistical calculations to predict the predicament awaiting the group at the end of the year. Unfortunately, it was not easy to decide on which weekly activities to drop in the interest of education.

If the group needed a kick on the side to change their focus, then Dr Kamau was the perfect one to deliver this.

Dr Kamau was entrusted with the responsibility for sharpening the eyes for the microscopic detail of the human body. "He took the responsibility too seriously," was the unanimous assessment by all the groups of students.

To underscore this, Dr Kamau one day demanded to know from the students, "What does it matter whether the monkey hung upside down or leaped with great agility across empty space?"

"You will be treating human beings, not monkeys and baboons," was his advice.

Every Friday Dr Kamau administered a sport test where each student had to correctly identify ten body organs by examining tissue under the microscope. For each student he plotted a line graph of marks attained on consecutive weeks. At a critical moment when the line took a steep decline and was dangerously close to zero point, he summoned the unfortunate student to his office and instructed the student to examine the trend line of the marks. He would then pose the question, "At this rate where will the line end?"

He would not be expecting an answer but his long and serious look drove the point home. No one required more than two visitations with Dr Kamau to recognise that there was eminent risk at the end of the academic cliff. In any event, no student fancied a confrontation with the sadist Noguchi who determined one's fate in the anatomy studies at the end of the year. Noguchi was one of the external examiners who provided the yardstick for quality assurance on the school's standards.

Noguchi had chided one unfortunate student who dared give him two consecutive wrong answers, "Did you attend all the anatomy sessions during the year?" the interrogation ran.

"Yes, sir," answered the student.

"Then you wasted your father's time and money, you would have done better looking after your father's cattle," Noguchi lamented before concluding the interview with the verdict, "see you next season."

This meant that the student would "rewind", as the students called repeating the entire year's courses or joining the class behind.

To another student he advised, "In the interests of time, if you do not know the answer to my questions just say, 'I don't know' so we can pose another question."

The unfortunate victim made comfortable by this assurance, continued to give the same answer, "I don't know," to three consecutive questions.

Furious, Professor Noguchi cautioned, "Young man, if you continue saying 'I don't know' to every question, then we will believe you!"

Fortunately, for Masaii, three visits to Dr Kamau's office and sordid tales from an encounter with Noguchi did the trick.

The final blow was when Dr Kamau posted a chilling reminder on the school notice board. The message read, "Please watch it, during your final examinations at the end of this year don't be like the student who on making microscopic examination of tissues mistook the liver for bone marrow, the spleen for liver, the lung for connective tissue and the uterus, he called the heart."

Such errors, Dr Kamau had warned, indicated that the student was not fit to be a doctor and the examiners would willingly oblige him in this request!

It is at this moment precisely two months before the final examination that Masaii could clearly see his mission to become the demigod slipping away. He embarked on his studies with a passion.

***

"I am John Odhiambo Opar, Man of Letters", a cranky, amiable six-foot tall introduced himself to a group of new students, before falling into an extended bark of hacking laugher. His was the kind of laughter that a fellow student once described to be "the maniacal laughter of a triumphant hyena".

John Odhiambo Opar or simply Man of Letters as he preferred to be called, was a friend to all and a great inspiration to many of his colleagues. He adored books and learning in general, not just the study of medicine. It is this love for knowledge that earned him the title, or more correctly justified him to take on the title, "Man of Letters".

Man of Letters had acquired a shoulder drop on his right hand which he called "the academic angle of inclination", amid the characteristic laughter.

One acquired this angle through many years of intimacy with books, he explained to Masaii one day.

He went on to demonstrate the reason why medical students in particular would in due course develop a greater angle than any other student on campus by bringing out Harrison's Textbook of internal medicine, which is at least five kilograms heavy. He then added the textbook of surgery by Bailey and Love before inviting Masaii to examine these heavy books and telling him that his great angle of inclination could not be explained on the basis of the load.

"Look at the 'Penguins,'" (as he called the students studying Literature) they have zero emphasis on "the angle of inclination!"

He called them "Penguins" because of the drawing of a penguin appearing on the cover of each of the classics that students of languages read.

Of course the students taking these courses were not amused by this dubious title and so on one of these days when Man of Letters arrived late from the pub inebriated and loquacious, one Penguin decided enough was enough and with one left, floored John Odhiambo Opar. On this day, Man of Letters had been to the popular joint known as 'Matunda'. Here at the entrance was inscribed in bold 'Liquids of Wisdom: Wines and Spirits'. It is here that Man of Letters, intent on "washing his nephrons" as he called beer drinking, had had a little too much to take on the fateful day. When one of the students at the halls of residence warned him to stop disturbing him as he was studying for the next day's examination, Man of Letters, with his unique laughter now highly accentuated by alcohol, retorted, "Shut up you Penguin, how dare you show disrespect to the only scholar on this floor!"

It is at the Matunda where Man of Letters had been once arrested and charged with creating a disturbance.

"And what exactly did the accused do that you call, 'causing a disturbance'?" the magistrate demanded from the prosecuting police officer.

"Your honour, the accused walked into the bar full of airs, as if all the other patrons present did not exist or matter," the officer described the reasons why Man of Letters was in the dock.

"Your honour, the people in the pub, including the arresting officer, took great exception to the condescending and pompous attitude of the accused," explained the prosecutor. "Your honour, hell broke loose when the accused demanded to know who it was that was occupying the seat reserved only for the Man of Letters".

With a smile, the magistrate released Man of Letters with the advice, "You need a degree in humility."

It was about this time that John Odhiambo Opar defined rape as "crush landing in thigh-land", much to the hilarity of the fellow students and sheer bewilderment of the ageing British Professor of Internal Medicine.

During the five years in the college, in his deportment Man of Letters oscillated between buffoonery and genius while his posture assumed a permanent drooping of the left shoulder, a consequence of the ever-increasing "academic angle of inclination".

"I will be a surgeon," the Man of Letters predicted with such conviction that no one ever doubted him.

Masaii wondered how he could be so sure when he had not even graduated from the medical school.

"Look at my fingers, they are the fingers of a surgeon," explained John Odhiambo Opar amidst a most garish laughter.

For what appeared to be an eternity, Masaii listened with keen interest as Man of Letters apportioned surgical responsibilities to each of his fingers least of all the left index finger, "that would make clinical excision of the prostate with one clean sweep round the inside of the bladder neck!" This would be after the right index finger had determined that the prostatic enlargement was of non-cancerous nature through an equally precise rectal examination.

John Odhiambo Opar explained all these with his eyes closed as if in a trance.

Besides being a good student and a source of inspiration to others, John Odhiambo Opar possessed the rare quality of enjoying whatever he happened to be doing – a quality that he retained throughout his career as a surgeon and administrator at the regional hospital.

***

During his first year at the medical school, Masaii maintained what he called a balanced lifestyle, meaning keeping out of trouble despite the many opportunities to join the rioting students in pelting the police with stones.

However, on at least one occasion he was in real danger of expulsion when he joined the boys in some impish prank. One such episode involved Man of Letters and a young sociology female student nicknamed Tieni. To describe Tieni as extraordinary would be an understatement. Tieni was different from all the girls in college. Tieni was naughty beyond measure, with no sense of obscenity or indecency – everything was fun and there is no fun if it isn't shared! So on one day Tieni challenged all the boys to a sexual duel! She described herself as a heavy "bomber" that would outdo any of the novices on campus. Man of Letters, intent on proving that he was not merely a bookworm, presented himself as the match for Tieni.

A day was set for the duel. As the day approached, the tension and excitement was feverish. Masaii was among the many students flocking the hall of residence where the competition was to take place.

John Odhiambo Opar showed himself at the third floor balcony next to his room, doing a macho romp adorned with his characteristic laughter. They did not have long to wait for Tieni, as she arrived clad in short pants and promptly received loud applause from the boys and girls milling around the corridors. The excitement was palpable.

Masaii was enjoying his favourite drink at Blukat – a famous hangout for university students when the legendary Josiah Mwangi Kariuki (or JM as he was popularly known) walked in and soon the enthusiastic students in attendance invited themselves to his table.

JM had a magnetic presence wherever he happened to be. University students were particularly vulnerable to his presence. It was therefore no surprise that his arrival caused the re-arrangement of tables so that the students could rub shoulders with JM, the Member of Parliament from Nyandarua.

The magic effect JM's presence had on the revellers led Masaii to propose a "beauty index", as he called it.

"When you are in a function and a lady walks in," Masaii instructed his colleagues, "if you want to know if the lady is beautiful, don't look at her but survey the reaction of the men in the audience." The reaction of the men is a measure of the beauty in the new arrival.

Masaii did not know that this was to be the first and last time for him to experience the charm and munificence of JM. Nor did Masaii realise how this politician would affect his own life more so in his untimely death.

The discussion with JM centred on injustices of the Kenyatta Government; how the regime exploited the downtrodden masses and the poor. This was a favourite subject among the young intellectuals at the university.

Otonglo was animated as he expounded on Karl Marx and Hengels. A discussion like this would not end without the famous call to the masses to arise "for you have nothing to lose except your chains!"

JM was an icon of resistance and the ideal Member of Parliament. He exuded self-confidence and a vision for a paradise on earth and specifically in Kenya where there was no suffering from want. He was convinced and did not miss an opportunity to expound on the thesis. "If the government performed and was transparent then poverty would be banished from within the borders of Kenya" was the recurring theme of this kind of encounter with JM. On this occasion JM reminded them of their obligations to society but most significantly for the students was his declaration: "You are the future leaders!"

These were no ordinary times in Kenya. Jomo Kenyatta ruled the country like an invisible but ever-present colossus. His favourite rhetoric was '*Tutawaponda ponda kama unga*'. Meaning, "We shall crush (grind) dissidents to pulp – or, more accurately – maize flour!"

The definition of a dissident was most elastic and the more-than-eager state security ruthlessly meted punishment to would-be dissidents at the primordial stage. It is this regime that introduced draconian laws in the country such as detention without trial. Anybody who dared oppose the regime or what it represented, either served an indefinite detention term or, as in the case of JM, in the 'Hall of the Inexplicable Deaths'. In this he joined Pio Gama Pinto, Makhan Singh, Tom Mboya and a long chain of lesser mortals felled by an assassin's bullet.

"If this man has not done anything for you as your Member of Parliament, then don't vote for him (JM)," ran the front page of JM's election manifesto. With the circulation of the brief manifesto, JM eluded the campaign period in the country, choosing to visit one of the South East Asia economic tigers. Such was the poise of the man, and little wonder that in this, his last election, he won with probably the largest landslide vote in the country, a win only rivalled by that of the legendary Jaramogi Oginga Odinga (OO) or simply double 'O' as he was fondly referred to.

JM's death was truly a political tsunami in Kenya.

The death of JM was the hallmark of the Jomo Kenyatta legacy. Intrigue, murder and gentle extortion was the legacy of Jomo.

"Kenya is a man-eat-man society," declared Julius Nyerere of Tanganyika.

For one hundred days, the country burnt. There were riots at the beach, in the city streets and in the villages.

JK was silent.

It was rumoured that he was on board a ship in the Indian Ocean, ready to leave the country for an unknown destination.

Others concluded "he is the legendary Otwori the caveman".

He has receded to the caves of Mount Kenya, was the common belief. Salimo lived through the JK era as one in a dream.

In his view, during this time one belonged to one of four groups. The first group was the ruling class; no more than a dozen members of the gang, or Kamaliza as students called it, living the JK life. They breathed the air that JK breathed, lived his life, drunk his black coffee and sang his songs. When he was on the famous busy working holiday in Mombasa, which was all the days except when he was opening the sham parliament, listening to the phony budget or reading presidential speeches on the three public holidays of Independence Day, Kenyatta Day or The Madaraka Day. They were his errand boys, the enforcers and de facto rulers. Woe unto you if you crossed the path of these untouchables, particularly one who had acquired the name of Kissinger!

Kissinger knew the meaning of his master's gestures. All the boss had to do is raise his hand or name some miscreant.

JM was a victim of the gang.

The second group consisted of the idiot servants who served the regime. This included the lifelong team of civil servants JK inherited from the colonial government. Many of them considered traitors in the struggle for independence became the loyal servants of their new master. These were two dozen or so but they controlled the government, holding it in a firm grip like their boss held his chief's fimbo (cane)!

The two groups were the government.

When Nyerere talked of the man-eat-man society, these were the ones cannibalising everybody else in the country.

The next were the intellectuals and seven parliamentary mavericks commonly known as the seven bearded sisters!

The life of an intellectual then was that of fear of the dreaded state security machinery or that of exile in neighbouring countries. If long-term exile was a reality, they migrated further south to Zimbabwe and when Mugabe threw a political convulsions, they journeyed to the homelands of South Africa, the United States of America or Australia – hot on the trails of the migrating colonial farmers. From these safe political havens they continued to foul JK air with literary curses. As JK never read this kind of literature, this was only of limited effect.

Later in Eritrea, Salimo understood of the philosophy of these exiles. It is the respite of a woman in labour, who when she farts believes that she has given birth!

Salimo and his gang formed the other group of the 'disgruntled elements'. Among this were students and lesser politicians.

These four groups were the politically conscious ones.

Everybody belonged to the masses who, depending on who they supported of the ruling class, received handouts. You were doomed if you sided with the intellectuals or students.

When JM disappeared, the man-eaters, including the top journalists colluded to hide the truth until Ole Tunda the Maasai herdsman chanced on the mutilated body deep in the Ngong forest! Some days before the disappearance of JM, government agents had planted a bomb in a public transport bus in a failed attempt to link JM to the crime.

Student riots only earned Salimo one more year in college as the university was closed for one year.

When JK emerged from his hideouts, two awesome and noisy low-flying F-17 fighter jets sent hundreds of walkers in Nairobi City running for safety.

When the report of the parliamentary select committee investigating the disappearance and murder of JM presented its mutilated report, Salimo made sure he was one of those in the public gallery shouting shame every time a finger was pointed at the government. As was to be expected, the ruling class muscled the parliament and nothing has been heard of any arrests of the criminals! The JM case is destined to eternally live in the museum of the unexplained murders and disappearances!

Salimo had met JM once at Blukat, a downtown joint which the politician frequented and freely mingled with intellectuals and students.

JM was a victim of motion. He moved and mingled with the wrong groups. The ruling classes feared any movement. The actions, motions and views of such a marked man were monitored and his movements watched. He did not watch out for Machiavelli's words: as the Prince, the people should either love you or fear you. He dared not fear or endear himself with the ruling class.

At Blukat, JM had paid for a couple of beers for Salimo and his friends.

You, my reader may have realised that it is not quite true – what I have said of the fate intellectuals. There were two other options. Detention without trial was a favourite of the regime. The other, less successful one, was that of playing the cat-and-mouse game with the state security. Only OO was ever so successful using this strategy.

As a senior medical student, Salimo played his role; that of treating fellow students who were tortured, raped or victims of random violence by the police.

Salimo would ensure that the students received their discharge from the ward before the police came to pick them for "interrogation", which was the euphemism used for further torture.

Detention as a weapon of repression and was perfected in the Moi regime. This is when the dungeons in the city centre were constructed.

Man is a restless animal, he is like water. He loves motion. You may confine him, torture him or terrorise his mind. The moment you release him, he runs. He is in search of another point to launch his action. Every pounding of the torturer's club was like forging iron. Many these 'dissidents' are as strong as steel but ever malleable! How else could one describe Raila Odinga or Madiaba?

It was after one such police incursion into the university that Salimo had spent the whole night attending to the injured students, failing to read the text on six causes of an enlarged spleen.

"Knowledge is not congenital, knowledge is acquired," his professor of internal medicine explained, to underscore why a medical student must read.

"A medical student cannot sleep before midnight," Serumaga went on to expound on the miserable life of a student.

For the next semester, Salimo, John Odhiambo and Obush took turns to enact the mini lecture:

Knowledge is acquired!
Knowledge is not congenital

Salimo remembers these sessions to this day. He remembers the day the psychiatrist declared internists to be robots! When they can explain the condition they recommend "repeat the blood test!" Muhanji was an academician, master of rhetoric and politician. He had the evidence with which he condemned the internists – five meters of electrocardiograph tests. The patient suffered from anxiety and instead of the internists listening to the patient, they ordered repeated ECG tests, as this is commonly referred to. Reading is not enough, thinking is even more important.

Muhanji was a darling of the students. He made psychiatry a science. All mental illnesses have a neurological basis, he would state. This was before ending the message with his usual sentence that started with, "this therefore". Finally he would adjust his trouser that was always threatening to drop for no other reason than that he frequently stood on one leg like a Maasai herdsman.

Some think JK was Kenya's messiah, but many consider him sly, a fox in sheep's skin! What would you call a leader who amassed so much power and wealth when those people he claims to have been fighting for were barely having a meal for the day, including the few he had not displaced from his rural palatial home?

Salimo attended the post-mortem of the unknown African, with several front teeth knocked out to disguise him as one from the lake region.

The murderers had no time to version a foreskin to complete the act of disfigurement! People have a preference for short-term decisions over their long-term interests. Were these mandarins pursuing their short-term gain, thereby grossly discounting our common good? Or were they operating on the principle: mine is mine but yours we share?

***

"What is the diagnosis of your patient?" Jean, the square-headed classmate, wanted to know.

"He has an enlarged prostate, which he describes in dramatic detail. Apparently he was on a bus to his home village in Kisii when he was struck.

"He had just downed one Coca Cola and wanted to empty his bladder for the rest of the journey. But somehow there was only a trickle and when the flow resumed, it was like a shower, not the usual strong stream.

"He did not know what to make of it but once in the village the pain in his bladder was like fire.

"'I was somersaulting all over the compound,' he explains amid-mirth.

"He is very grateful and thankful for what he calls 'lifesaving and God-sent action', as he describes the needle puncture.

"He was not so grateful to me when I decided to pass the urethral catheter," Salimo continued.

"What case do you have?"

Jean was not so enthusiastic to answer but then added: "He has an everlasting erection." Salimo had not yet heard of this condition, but thought it was what every man wants. "It is painful," Jean protested, apparently offended that Salimo was not sympathetic. "Imagine, I, a virgin, being allocated as my first patient a case of priapism."

Salimo could no longer contain his long-suppressed laughter. Jean was the leader of the Christian Union. Salimo never doubted her claim to virginity.

"So what are you going to do for the patient?" Salimo enquired.

"I have tried sedation, as the condition is caused by anxiety, but is it not working. Our lecturer proposed that I make multiple punctures to let out the blood. I am not sure. Will you help me? How can I do this as my first clinical procedure?"

Salimo volunteered to help.

Later in the evening, this case was the source of many theories.

Obush explained that the patient may have used some aphrodisiac. "We have the plant in my village," he explained. "I understand the lady is the one who gave an overdose. She wanted to have a time of a lifetime!"

"Do you know, less than one woman in five have vaginal orgasms," Obush continued, at which point Jean stormed out of the room.

"I know why it happened" John offered to help. "These were stolen goods. The husband of the woman in question had consulted the witchdoctor from Ukambani.

Do you know the famous medicine man that came to cleanse the office of the old minister from Ukambani?"

A story was making the rounds on how the semi-illiterate minister in the government, not rusting his predecessors, had the office stripped off all fabrics – curtains, carpet and furniture and installed everything anew before inviting the medicine man to purify the place.

Such is the superstition in Ukambani that one must take protective measures before embarking on an important mission.

Muli remembers the day his uncle cancelled a trip to the city because he had sported Muli kicking the tyre to see if pressure was enough.

His uncle was furious. "How can you kick the wheel? This is sacrilege" his uncle had thundered.

According to Muli, in Ukambani, sex was important and so there is medicine for enhancing performance. In fact, he added, being a virgin at marriage is frowned upon. If your bride turns out to be a virgin you are required to demand payment for lack of preparation. You are entitled to a one-cow fine.

"It is called installation of software," announced Obush, to the disgust of Tieni. "Yes, that is why you should be paid for the software and the installation," he continued.

"Tomorrow is theatre day for our urology unit," announced Muli, before departing to go and prepare the cases.

As a young doctor, final year students supposed, it was your responsibility to make sure all the pre-operation procedures were done. This was meant to ensure there was adequate blood, grouped and cross-matched. The patient should have had the consent given and if the anaesthetist's review unearthed cases like chest problems, high blood pressure or abnormal thyroid function, you made the consultations.

One of the patients suffered from penile cancer. He had to undergo amputation and radical excision. He required counselling and consent, which on previous occasions had proven difficult to obtain. There was some negotiation to be done.

***

Muli was not sure how to convince Chege to accept the amputation of his penis, or at least most of it. Chege had recently developed a growth in the most precious organ; as he described it. This had made it difficult to have relations with his three wives. The only treatment offered him a reasonable chance of a cure, provided the excision was wide enough. He was afraid the cure for cancer would ruin his life as he was sure his wives would leave him. "What is the use of man who is without his sexual function?" he would ask.

"How much would you cut off?" The negotiation had started.

"This much," Muli replied, indicating the length with his middle finger, which was almost at the base.

"That is the whole thing!" lamented Chege. "I will become a woman, I will have to squat to pass urine. What will become of me?" Several heads popped out of the bed covers to fathom the disaster that was to befall their most entertaining guest.

"But this is the only chance that you have with this kind of disease," explained the doctor. "In the worst-case scenario, that is if you delay, we may have to remove even the testis," continued the doctor. "We call this wide excision."

Covering his face with both hands, Chege mourned, "I know it! I have heard it. I am to be converted to an old woman!"

"We don't want to change you into anything that you don't want, we only want to help you live longer," continued the doctor, trying to remain inaudible to the line of heads attentively listening.

"Alright, but promise to leave this much," Chege begged. He indicated how much should be left behind. This was all but the one inch or so that he would sacrifice.

"Only this much for your life," Muli wondered. "That will not do. We would leave all the dangerous cells behind. The disease has extended up to here. And we have to leave a margin of error."

"Then let me go home," implored Chege.

"Think about it," Muli suggested, as he prepared to leave for the night.

Even as he signed the consent form, Dr Muli was not quite sure of the actual demarcation of the excision. But he was happy that he had obtained the consent. The rest will be left to the surgeon who would be performing the operation. Mr Muya, the urologist, would be the surgeon.

Mr Muya was the most renowned urologist in the country. In fact, he was the only one in the country. He had trained at Makerere during the colonial days. He was the first in everything. The only one from his village who escaped the colonialist embargo imposed on the Kikuyu tribe for their armed rebellion. Mau activity was its peak when Muya was of school-going age. During the theatre days, Muli and his colleagues relished the operation day. Mr Muya preferred the English custom that mandated that surgeons be referred to as "Mister" and not Doctor.

"Surgeons are physicians who can also perform surgical procedures," he would explain. "We are super physicians," was his usual conclusion to any discussion about the medical disciplines.

During the morning of the excision, Mr Muya was full of life and many anecdotes.

"Do you know that on some days we could not go to school? When the operations against the Mau Mau were intense, we would be warned to stay at home. One day we did not receive the message and were on our way to school when we heard the dreaded Land Rover and commotion in the market place. We hid in a small thicket from where we could see the green vehicle and the agitated village people, including my father. The Land Rover was dragging a corpse, one of the felled Mau Mau terrorists, as they were branded!" Mr Muya paused here to let us picture the scene.

"That night all males of age were rounded up and transferred to the isolation camp. The dreaded camp until then was reserved for the arrested known Mau Mau fighters. There was a ringed fence all round it. The prisoners had dug a trench of about twenty meters which was filled with water to prevent them from escaping. To access the camp there was a single drawbridge that was removed at night for safekeeping.

"Dawn-to-dawn curfew was imposed which usually was twenty four hours for men folk. Women could go out briefly during the daytime to fetch water, food or firewood.

"I remember once when I was on holiday from Makerere, the dawn-to-dawn curfew was declared. During this ultimate curfew, colonial soldiers would shoot at any moving object. So nobody dared outside. I was the only one at home with my mother. I decided to dig the pit latrine in the house. We had some food and water. Then my mother went into labour on one of the nights. I could not go out to call for help. Fortunately this was during my fourth year of medical studies and so I had done my course on obstetrics and gynaecology."

Mr Muya once more paused for us to comprehend the scene. "Imagine me conducting labour for my mother!"

"I think we have to perform radical excision for this patient's penis and surrounding tissues," he announced as he concluded his narration of the ordeals he had to endure during the period the emergency decade in Kenya.

"Forget about the home guards in Kenyatta's regime!" Mr Muya warned. "*Kwenye mbio sa mamba pia huwemo kenge!*" he concluded, using the Kiswahili proverb that translates to "in the race of crocodiles even giant lizards participate".

***

"Please fill in for me the next two days and I will return the favour". That was Dr Muli as an intern appealing to Salimo to cover his shifts for the weekend.

Throughout the university days, Muli somehow managed to pull stunts and surprises. The next two days meant the entire weekend! Also in his characteristic manner during the time of tabling the request he already had his suitcase packed and was on his way out. In this way, he made the request impossible to turn down. There was no time to negotiate!

On some odd occasions, Muli would really pull through breath-taking feats!

Take the occasion when a patient arrived and was rushed into the emergency department with overt symptoms of drug side effects. After resuscitation and recovery, the patient volunteered the information that a "Dr Muli" was his doctor and that he had prescribed the medication. The patient also indicated that Dr Muli was even one of the resident doctors in the hospital and regularly visited him as he was recuperating. "Dr Muli has his part-time clinic in Eastleigh," the patient explained. The description of a doctor with white hair, good sense of humour and not too old despite the hair changes was a perfect fit for Muli.

Later in the day when Salimo and his other fellow students confronted Muli, he was very apologetic and swore by all gods on the land that he had closed the "clinic" after this "unforgettable" incident.

"One has to make a living," Muli explained, before providing a graphic description of his family circumstances.

Taking off his shirt, he went into great detail to describe when and how he received the scars on his chest and head. They were all from the many encounters with the local police and the local chief who, intent on stumping out illicit brews, usually tortured the victims. The torture was not supposed to be a deterrent but to extort some money out the prisoners. "You see, I paid my way into university using income earned from brewing and selling *Changaa*!" Muli explained.

Changaa is the illicit spirit brewed in the villages and a source of frequent skirmishes in the villages whenever the chief made the regular raids for additional income.

"Do you see this long scar on my thigh? This one is from an injury incurred flying over the barbed wire at the chief's camp. My athletic prowess has saved me from tight corners, particularly escaping from custody," Muli concluded.

Muli then went on to heap praises on the Jomo Kenyatta government for providing free university education and on top of it, providing him with a boom. Unfortunately, Jomo was not generous enough and "one had to supplement the income from other sources".

Of all the things Masaii hated as a young doctor, topmost on the list was performing autopsies. He disliked this in the same way he hated being present when corporal punishment was being administered in the local prison. It was a requirement that a doctor be present to certify that the prisoner was fit to withstand the punishment. Even worse was the torture of being available at the execution to assure the authorities that there was no other medical cause of death except the execution itself.

Despite his antipathy for these mundane services as he called them, from time to time he derived humour from his indulgence.

The previous night he had been called upon to attend to a delicate police matter. The police sergeant wanted him to examine a male couple who had been caught "red-handed having unnatural sex in a public car park". The doctor's evidence would be crucial in obtaining a conviction.

"Sergeant, in the medical school, gay sex was not part of our forensic pathology course," he protested.

"What did you do?" asked Muli.

"The easiest way out, I referred the case to the only trained forensic pathologist one hundred kilometres away."

"Do you know what happened?" Muli wanted to know the full story.

"No," explained Masaii. "All I know is that it was next to impossible to get this particular pathologist out of bed, let alone the comfort of his home. He would invent every kind of excuse for the morgue to leave him alone.

On one occasion, he was called late in the night to come and draw a sample of blood from a drunken driver who had knocked down a late night reveller."

"Officer," he protested, "I am probably equally as drunk as that poor motorist, if not more!"

"But some of the cases are outright hilarious," Masaii went on to describe another recent event, its news was still circulating in his home village of Sengera long after the event.

One of them related to a prominent businessman who died while having intercourse with a young damsel, as Masaii called teenage girls.

The honourable gentleman had visited a home where he was to render services. It was rumoured that while being shown around the farmland that his workmen would be tilling the next day, he went on to seduce the farmer's daughter. There being no better place than the green mattress, as John Odhiambo Opar would call it, the couple decided to obey their thirst there and then. Unknown to them, the farmer's wife had dispatched her youngest son to deliver a juicy-looking chicken to the randy businessman and express their apology for not being able to provide a meal as culture required. In the small village, the frontier between business and friendship was thin. It all amounted to a relationship.

It was in the course of making the delivery that the young man spied on the two rascals, as they came to be known in the aftermath of the misadventure.

Sensing that he had chanced upon one of those cardinal sins that exterminate the sinners and witnesses without distinction, the young man let go of the cock as he ran for his life in horror. On hitting the ground the poor cock marked its freedom with a joyous cry as it flew into the woods. Whether it is the cry from the rooster or the shock of being discovered it was reported that the damsel heaved off the lover as she sped off in the opposite direction. As for the poor man; the events were too much for him! He died instantly on landing with the all his 'tools' undeterred. Forensic science reveals that when a victim dies in fright, the entire body goes into spasms, preserving all the evidence. This is what happened to the poor man! The immediate problem for the first responders was how to accommodate his erect member in his trousers.

Such was the shame that mourners this time broke with tradition to condemn such behaviour, especially from the elderly men who in any event, could not cope with the demands of the hot-blooded teenagers!

As for the girl, her ordeal was far from over. As demanded of the law in cases of sudden death, this should be subject of coroner's enquiry. As the last person to see the deceased alive, she was detained in local police cells for questioning. However, several days of questioning did not reveal any wilful involvement in the demise of the businessman.

"My Lord," she informed the presiding judge, "I did not know that he would soon be checking out."

She was fully exonerated when the physician who knew the businessman, informed the court that the deceased suffered from severe cardiac arrhythmia and was due to go abroad for a pacemaker.

Spiced…collection…demolishing the embarkment.

Muli was, in the view of Salimo, the proverbial cat with nine lives, at least in his long road to becoming a doctor. As a medical student he believed in doing just enough to make the grade.

"To enjoy work, you must 'spice' it" was his philosophy. He was usually the epicentre of drama as a student. He was one of the student leaders who had to complete their medical studies in Dar es Salaam, having been expelled for anti-government activities. He was the Minister for Social Affairs in the student government.

His expulsion was anything but political. Two events contributed to this. Firstly, he was at the centre of a sexual harassment incident only he was capable of both designing and executing.

One Sunday evening, he had gone out to the joint popularly known to the student community as Matunda. It derived its name from the Jomo Kenyatta call to all Kenyans to enjoy the fruits of independence. "It is your fault if you choose to wallow in poverty instead of enjoying the fruits of independence," the founding father would warn political activists and more so the student leadership that was growing more cynical and radical by the day.

Matunda was therefore the place one could harvest low-lying fruits at a student rate. On this particular Saturday, Muli presented himself as a foreign student from Zambia.

After the first round of drinks he passed on the bill to his date with the excuse that he had no shillings (the local currency) but was a student tycoon in Kwachas. The deal was that once he converted these into shillings she would take leave from Matunda for the year. She could even travel with him on holiday to see the mighty Victoria Falls.

After an overly successful Sunday out, the couple agreed to proceed to his room at the university campus, where he would repay the lady for the courtesies in monetary terms, and also in kind. His date, now referred to as the "collection", obliged and proceeded to order a taxi for which she also settled the bill.

Well rewarded in the flesh (but not financially), they set out to walk back to town so she could go to her home. They could not call a cab as the red booth was not working. There were no cell phones either.

As they were about to bid farewell, Muli suddenly 'remembered' that he had not 'brought' the Kwachas. So they decided to walk back to his campus room. It was during the second visit to the room that things started to go horribly wrong.

Firstly, upon arrival, Muli excused himself and left to wash his "nephrons" so he could have a late morning as there was no point for the date to leave. They could spend Sunday recovering together. This was a most welcome prospect coming at around five o'clock in the morning.

The previous night's exhaustion did not dull the senses of the young lady to the extent that she could not detect that the one who returned into bed was not Muli but some other stranger!

She raised the alarm, not knowing that this was all planned. Muli as a good comrade was merely sharing his fruits!

It is not clear whether it was Muli or the classmate who shouted "collection", to which call all the males in the hostel emerged, raring for a taste of the fruit! They arrived in numbers, some in their undergarments, others with all manners of wrap-arounds!

Within a minute of the shout "collection", the room was invaded and the young lady found herself in the courtyard, the remains of her clothing shredded into minute pieces. Some only wanted to touch the "goods". Such was the ruckus that the police had to intervene to save the poor lady. Salimo offered her his T-shirt, fortunately this was plain white with no messages such as "make love not war", that were popular in the campus those days.

For many days, Obush relished every minute of this "sensuous feast" as he called it. "I could not wash this left hand of mine for the entire week", he would announce to all who cared to listen. They carried the aroma from the "goods", and he would proudly display all the five fingers of his right hand.

The university took a very dim view of this event and Muli was suspended from the Halls of Residence.

This was one of the many incidents that would characterise Muli's academic life at the university. The one which broke the camel's back was his attempt to demolish the barrier above the underground tunnel that prevented students and pedestrians from crossing the road, forcing them to use the tunnel under the road.

The construction of the pedestrian tunnel was the culmination of many years of skirmishes and confrontations between the students who feared for their lives each day they the crossed the busy street. Such skirmishes would spike at examination time or whenever there was a hot issue such as suspected political assassination. On such occasions, it would be absolute mayhem. Motorists would be at the receiving end with broken screens and car windows. The bloodshed would only be brought to an abrupt end by the inevitable announcement that the Senate of the university had closed the institution indefinitely, followed by the invasion of the university campus by the dreaded general services unit, a special police or paramilitary unit whose brutality knew no limit, rape being the most preferred method of putting down rebellion, as they saw it.

The aftermath of such events could best be compared to weeks after the devastation of New Orleans after Hurricane Katrina. The bloodstained street would be littered with broken glass, a glut of stones and wreckage of burnt cars – a scene to be matched with the broken doors and windows at the university hostel.

Ironically, once the tunnel was constructed "at great cost", as Jomo Kenyatta would lament, students would not use it, preferring to weave through the busy street above, forcing the government to construct a concrete barrier above.

In time, the barrier became a source of recurrent stoning of speeding cars and a nuisance both to the government and students. It was this concrete barrier that Muli one day was determined to bring down blow after blow, "however long it took!" forcing the university to permanently terminate his registration.

In life, as one grows older you encounter all kinds of conmen!

The one conman who took Salimo's breath away was Sam, a conman who never let any piece of action slip through his fingers. Usually Sam left the victim more amused than angry.

Sam was a legend of many stunts in his fight against poverty. Even in Salimo's wildest imaginations he never suspected that he would be a victim of Sam. But no one was immune. On this occasion Sam decided that the best way to get something back from the government was to use its means, especially using the government vehicle to hoist some merchandise without the police interfering. Firstly he had to acquire a government vehicle. This is when Sam decided that he would play the role of a doctor, a pathologist.

"Doctor, doctor," the head nurse was ecstatic!

"Come and welcome our new pathologist," said Dr Masaii.

Salimo was not prepared for the gentleman presented to him. He was very smartly dressed in a three-piece black suit, white shirt and yellow tie. His shoes were so clean that one could use them for a mirror!

He announced with a flair, "I am a newly-posted pathologist to the district."

As the district medical officer, that was the greatest news one could receive. This was Christmas come early. For the DMO among the many things that he never liked to do is frequenting the District Morgue.

The place was run-down, it was dilapidated beyond description. It was like – if government cannot fully care for the living, why worry about the dead!

At Salimo's hospital, only the morgue attendant, Johanna relished being around his "super office", as he called the place.

"It is the super office because the rich and the poor must pass through this station to their final resting place," he would explain.

For the government to consider and send a pathologist to this difficult-to-reach place was the greatest thing that had happened to Salimo.

Abandoning all clinical duties, Salimo immediately embarked on locating a befitting office for "my most-preferred member of staff", as the newly posted pathologist was fondly referred to during his short tour of duty in the district.

In the meantime, Sam was booked into the best guesthouse where he would be spending the first two weeks in the new station, as prescribed by the law and procedures of the ministry.

Sam was then allowed three days to feel welcomed, look around and to start knowing the new place of his posting.

A few days later, Salimo decided to take him around the hospital and show him the great place it was. They started from the operations theatre, where Salimo worked, then the wards, the outpatient department and the residence for trainee nurses.

At the end of the week, Salimo enlisted the services of one of their drivers and serviced their most reliable long chassis Land Rovers to take him to the city to bring his household goods and his beloved wife, as he referred to her. As a comrade, Salimo had no reason to prevent this respectable man from enjoying the best in life.

Salimo released the driver, giving him sufficient money for his own wellbeing before allowing him to take the pathologist to the city so he could bring his family. However, before he left, Salimo requested the great pathologist to go and perform a post-mortem examination for the family who would be travelling almost 500 km to the shores of Lake Victoria. In this part of the world, the dead were immensely revered; more than the living. The villagers would sell the last chicken to raise the money to bring the body of the deceased back home. In commiseration with the bereaved, the DMO would have no reason to delay them because they needed to be home before dusk. They ensured arrival before nightfall, when dark forces start to play tricks on the living; as this might hinder a more civil process of delivering the body to the beloved ones.

So with this in mind, Salimo instructed the pathologist to speedily conduct the post-mortem examination. He was to set off as soon as the procedure was accomplished.

One week, then two weeks passed before the pathologist or the driver returned. This did not bother, Salimo given the importance of the guest.

However, during the third week Salimo started to worry that something was not right. He decided to call the ministry headquarters at the human resource department to find out what took the pathologist so long to come back.

To his surprise, he had hardly completed the sentence before he could hear a tornado of laughter on the end of the line! The explosive laughter could be heard in the great Uhuru Park!

When the party on the other end had recovered he explained to them what had transpired. They consoled Salimo and encouraged him not to worry, to be understanding that the world was full of conmen!

Their suggestion was to keep waiting, at least for the driver but in the meantime to lodge the matter with the police.

About one week later the driver arrived, thoroughly demoralised and dejected. He then narrated the story of what had transpired soon after they left the station, much to the amusement of the staff.

His story was brief. This was a scam.

The pathologist had offered to drive during part of the long journey to the "city". He remembers that he went to sleep and the next morning when he went to check on the pathologist as he had failed to turn up for breakfast, he found the room empty and the car not in the parking lot. There was no information even with the reception. He decided to wait for a few days before he could hitchhike from the lonely resort where he had been abandoned. It took the driver two weeks of hitchhiking from a neighbouring country where he had been abandoned, before he could find help in nearby township.

Later, when Salimo went to read the findings of the post-mortem examination, he was horrified to read the cause of death: "starvation", was the conclusion!

This was when he realised the magnitude of deception.

The Land Rover was later found abandoned at the border to the neighbouring country. Sam was never to be seen or heard of for the next three to four years!

His next episode was no less sinister. The man was never short on trickery.

This time Sam conjured up a plan to go to a neighbouring country where clothing materials or bedspreads were rumoured to be cheap but of high quality.

His next victims were two unsuspecting ladies from his village. He volunteered to be their guide or scout, as he was well travelled and highly connected.

Setting off in a double cabin Toyota four-by-four, they soon obtained the finest materials and merchandise at throwaway prices, as they said when they later narrated the story. Armed with their treasure, they drove back to the border and it was almost open to all and sundry. During these glorious days of East African Community there was almost free movement across East African states.

Anyway, they went through and bought some most fashionable materials that they could carry without arousing any suspicion with the customs officials on the Kenyan side of the border.

Sam dreamed of the idea that they could put the material in the bonnet of the car above the engine block. In this way the customs officers would not know or suspect anything.

Everything went according to plan except until the customs officer left to stamp their passports and they had nothing to declare.

As the officer was entering the next office for the stamping, he noticed something strange. There was a strange smell and he could see smoke ascending from engine. He ran back, calling on the occupants to move the car away from the building.

Calling out "bring some water or sand", the officers were frantic to save the car! "Open the bonnet of the truck," he was shouting to his colleagues.

The amount of commotion was enough to attract many onlookers.

In this part of the village, people are susceptible to drama and upon seeing smoke, soon there was a crowd of 200; all trying to salvage the car.

When the smoke and the dust settled, the officers could see remains of colourful clothing material that was now nearly reduced into ash. Of course the material and not the engine was the cause of the smoke and the fire.

Needless to say, the whole merchandise was confiscated and the conspirators were arrested and taken to a local holding cell. However, they appeared to be men and women of high means, so the police officers were willing to be lenient but they could not let them off scot-free.

They allowed them the luxury of sitting together to plan the next move. That is when the gentleman convinced the ladies that they pool together whatever monies they had so that they could raise sufficient funds for cash bail.

They could only raise just enough cash for just one person to be released. So it was argued that, since he was a man of the world and highly connected, he should be the one to go into the free world to look for help. But before he set off, he requested the officers to allow the one telephone call to a senior government official.

Once he mentioned that the Prime Minister was his uncle, they allowed the local governor.

"Sir, I am the son of the Prime Minister," he announced over the phone.

"I am in some small problem. Please do talk to my father and let him know that we are being held by the police.

"Let him know that we have been detained and we need his intervention." The governor was equally nervous as he called the Prime Minister.

"Sir, your son is detained here at my station," he informed the Prime Minster. "Sir what do you propose we do with them?" he asked.

The booming sound from the other end of the line was scary even to the Governor, once he mentioned the name of the PM's supposed son.

"Lock them up!" was the terse message.

"This thug has been going round destroying and defiling my name as well as the family name!" he warned.

When the thunderous noise was off the air, the governor enquired, "Young man, which one is your mother among the PM's wives?"

"Which one is your mother?" he repeated. This is when the truth came out.

"No, I am not his actual son but his nephew," he replied.

He was then told that the no help was forthcoming.

It was at this stage that the conspirators decided that now it was time for one of them to be out to seek for real salvation.

No sooner than Sam was barely free with a lawyer at hand, they were all out to attend court.

They were however not ruffled by the ensuing judgment which was: the truck and the merchandise were confiscated and to be auctioned.

To cut the story short, this conman still wanted to cut corners.

"Why hire an expensive lawyer when you can buy the judge?" he instructed my friend, the lawyer.

Unfortunately this particular lawyer did not believe in this philosophy so he declined the proposition; "kindly pay me for letting you out of the prison and get a lawyer who believes in your wayward ways."

This was not before Sam had tried to guide the lawyer on the line of questioning, preferring him not to ask tough questions that might complicate the case.

So, having been paid he excused himself and Sam was free to find a new lawyer.

The new lawyer requested for a certain sum for the presiding judge and the balance for himself.

However, the judgment did not go entirely their way.

The judge wanted to send a warning to criminals and gave a hefty fine or one year in prison.

Not surprisingly, however, Sam was not to be defeated.

Once the truck was at the auction, he arranged for a rich merchant in town to buy it back for the businesswomen.

Sam had proven once more that the road to riches is long and torturous. But, in his own words, to be rich one must continue moving, changing positions and evolving until one finds the right combination of the ingredients reaching this end. Soon thereafter, Salimo was visited by the legendary Yusufu.

This chance meeting with Yusufu turned out to be the beginning of a long-lasting friendship with Salimo. Yusufu was a man with a huge heart and a broad mind. He used to pride himself on the fact that he had escaped prosecution and eventual execution for allegedly plotting with unknown mercenaries to overthrow some Muslim country's government in northern Africa. He never hastened to add, "Bob was my saviour".

Bob was the illustrious Minister for Foreign Affairs who himself could not escape the cruel arm of unknown mercenaries who kidnapped him from his home and tortured him before setting his body on fire not too far from his village. This was a legacy of the regime of the country's founders and President.

From time to time, Yusufu never stopped narrating this incident. Indeed this near miss did not deter Yusufu from the mire of controversy. He never shied away from being at the centre of the world stage. He was not one to miss the chance to indulge in attempts to influence events, local and abroad.

"I will be going to Baghdad," he announced after a good dose of Indian biryani.

Once more, Yusufu had conjured the impossible idea of risking his life to attempt to broker a difficult peace deal between the Mullahs of Iran and Saddam Hussein as they engaged in a costly and inhuman war that left many dead on both sides and no winners; but worse still, that gave birth to a reign of terrorism in the region.

On his return, Yusufu narrated the sad tale of his failed but determined efforts to a group of Muslim scholars whom he was leading into Baghdad to meet with Saddam Hussein; to talk about peace in the name of Islam.

"My brother, Salimo," he concluded, "the man is mad," referring to Saddam Hussein. "Even as war raged in and around this region of the Middle East, we could not hold a reasonable and enlightened conversation with the man!" Completely out of his mind!" Needless to say, his efforts fell on deaf ears.

On this occasion, Yusufu was livid with the excitement. "Salimo, do you know that I saved Waruru Kanja from death?"

"I saved him from being hanged by the colonialists," he stated, beaming with moist eyes. "Do you know that Kanja was one of the foot soldiers for Mau Mau?" he asked.

"He was arrested and sent to the infamous Manyani Detention Camp overlooking the snow-peaked Mt Kilimanjaro.

During colonial days, being interned in Manyani was no different from being sent to the Russian Siberia or Gulag Archipelago. The vast desert surrounding the facility, teeming with all manner of wild animals around, including the man-eaters of Tsavo, effectively excluded possibility of successful escape. Indeed, throughout the lifetime of this detention camp, no detainee escaped. The only other way of leaving Manyani was if a prisoner was sentenced to death by hanging. This was what Waruru Kanja was waiting for on the fateful encounter with Yusufu.

The doctor's appointment with Yusufu, as the law required for the expert to testify, was one, so that the prisoner was fit for the capital punishment and secondly to ensure that death by hanging was the real cause of death and not some ubiquitous natural cause. In short, to be executed by hanging, the prisoner had to be at his best in health. The colonial government did not wish to be deprived of full restitutions of all the wrongs committed by the terrorist.

Therefore, on this morning the prisoner was brought into the doctor's surgery within the prison premises for the expert to give the green light to execute.

"On this occasion, I was the presiding physician," Yusufu explained.

"It is the one job I hated as a doctor," he continued. "No wonder I opted to become an obstetrician and gynaecologist later in life," Yusufu concluded.

Having interviewed and examined the prisoner, Yusufu satisfied himself that there was no pre-existing medical condition that might overtake hanging in causing the eventual demise of the prisoner. He then proceeded to examine the prisoner. He had created some rapport, having attended to this particular prisoner previously. Yusufu had found him to be an intellectual giant, a man of profound political conviction and truly revolutionary. Not a terrorist as alleged, but one consumed by the concern for social justice.

The term of social justice resonated very much with Yusufu's personal convictions. Yusufu was a man of social justice. No wonder he tried to broker a deal between two equally mad men on both sides of the Iraq-Iran conflict.

It did not escape Yusufu's conscious and innermost belief that according to his personal conviction, an innocent man should not be condemned to death!

"Not just because someone else did not share his views in relation to the welfare of fellow human beings, that is not enough reason to execute anybody," lamented Yusufu.

Therefore, having fully satisfied himself that the prisoner was absolutely healthy, Yusufu nevertheless had to find a reason to postpone their execution.

"You need to believe that tomorrow will always be better than today," Yusufu used to say.

"Salimo, I am one hundred percent optimistic," Yusufu continued. "You never know what tomorrow will bring," he deeply inhaled.

"Maybe as it has happened many years before Jesus Christ, the sun might be commanded to stop and thereby be brought to a standstill," Yusufu reflected as he continued with the story.

He then called for a thermometer and asked the prisoner to stick it into mouth. After a couple of minutes, he scrutinised the instrument carefully and in great detail and found the temperature of the prisoner to be below normal. Yusufu wanted to be absolutely sure and to take this into account as conclusive evidence that the prisoner was not in an optimum state of health. He decided to take the temperature again from another part of the body, the armpit.

Yes, indeed; the prisoner was running a temperature, he concluded. He then made a note in the prisoner's record. In the section marked for diagnosis, he recorded "Fever of Unknown Origin".

The doctor continued to make the categorical recommendation: Prisoner not fit for execution.

Yusufu proceeded to call the prison guards and requested them to send back this particular prisoner for he was running temperature.

Little did he know that these few degrees of temperature fluctuation could save a man's life, without any intervention!

Unknown to Yusufu, the colonial government had learned of the inhumane conditions prisoners were made to endure in detention camps. The colonial government in London had constituted a select committee to visit her Majesty's territories in Africa and investigate allegations of injustices committed against natives in detention camps, Manyani among them.

As fate would have it all, executions were to be postponed effective this day to await the outcome of the commission.

So during the following few days, new uniforms were issued to every detainee, the menu improved, their surroundings were made orderly, and the trees trimmed and manicured to make everything around Manyani look like paradise in that God-forsaken place.

Indeed, when the commission members visited the camp a few months later, they were impressed with the conditions existing in the prison. However, the general welfare of the prisoners did not escape their observation. Most prisoners appeared malnourished and many bore scars of the physical punishment. Therefore, despite the conditions existing on the day of the visit there was every reason to recommend immediate closure of the detention camp, with immediate release of all the prisoners.

"Indeed, that saved this great man," Yusufu recalled.

Later in life, Salimo met Waruru Kanja from time to time when he frequented Yusufu's private clinic to receive a weekly dose of the testosterone hormone injection to boost his performance, as he had recently acquired his fifth wife.

Kanja was a man of many lives. Neither Yusufu nor Kanja ever veered away from their conviction that social justice as a human value was of the highest order and probably fundamental to all great men.

Yusufu would now and then remind Salimo that this was the underlying message of Jesus Christ when he stated "Love you neighbour as you love yourself or love your enemy as you love yourself."

Usually, he would conclude: "Whether in Christianity, Islam or Buddhist faith, social justice is a central dictum."

No wonder Kanja would confound friend and foe when he cited social justice as the reason for him to come to the aid of a brother in need.

Kanja was being mentioned in a divorce petition where a spouse was alleging infidelity on the part of his wife as the reason for the rift.

When the affected husband was asked to call for witnesses, he called Kanja to the witness box.

"Honourable MP, did you ever have an affair with this woman?" asked the judge.

"Well, my Lord, I am an honest man," replied Kanja. "I have to admit that from time to time we have had moments of indulgence."

"Are you saying that you have been in liaison with this woman?"

"Yes, my Lord," replied Kanja.

With that pronouncement, there was a loud pounding on the table and the judge announced, "Divorce granted."

This happened much to the absolute annoyance and distraught of the affected woman, who considered this pronouncement. Indeed she could not restrain herself from venting her anger at the presiding judge.

"Conspiracy," she yelled.

"Miscarriage of justice!" she cried out.

At this juncture, the judge ordered that the woman be detained in police cells for contempt of court. Indeed, the two days and nights she was detained not only softened but mellowed her to the point that she could apologise and gain her freedom from both prison and her good-for-nothing or undeserving husband, as she described her former husband.

"All men are brothers," she concluded.

To Yusufu, Kanja was made of the same mantle as his compatriot Joseph Mwangi Kariuki, or simply JM as the country fondly referred to him.

JM Kariuki was equally fired up on the social justice paradigm.

JM was popular with not just medical students but with all university students. JM was a great man; popular with students. He was a defendant of the weak, a fighter for the poor and those who had been exploited. Indeed he was a brave and valiant warrior; one who would challenge even the greater Jomo Kenyatta.

The students frequently met JM from time to time at Blukat, a popular and inexpensive coffee house at Nairobi's Koinange Street. At Blukat, students would flock around JM in search of knowledge. They learned great wisdom and human experience first-hand from those who rubbed shoulders with Jomo Kenyatta.

It was a known fact that JM was the personal secretary to Jomo Kenyatta. Soon after independence, JM had grown huge wings and wanted to fly; and fly he did, landing at Nyandarua. The Nyandarua constituency lay at the foothills of Aberdares and was known to everybody in the country.

JM evoked the sweet memories of fighting for independence. He never stopped reminding Kenyans and in particular the ruling class why Mau Mau was formed; why Kenyans fought for independence.

JM would not fear to confront Jomo Kenyatta, even to tell to his face that the reason why Kenyatta was detained and the reason why many Kenyans died was as a result of fighting for justice and to have their stolen lands returned to them.

Not surprising that the regime found JM an irritant to the extent that he was kidnapped and his body was found a few weeks later at the foothills of Ngong Hills, not far from the Nairobi's Hilton Hotel deep in the city centre, where he was last seen having a drink with unknown persons.

The badly mutilated body with several teeth hacked out of his mouth to make him look like some God-forsaken Luo tribesman had been doused with some chemicals and set alight.

Unknown to the conspirators, this mischief prevented the hyenas from devouring the body, thus aiding identification.

The findings of the parliamentary committee investigating the death of JM were never published nor acted upon, as fingers were pointed from all directions at Jomo Kenyatta's regime. Prior to this, JM had been arrested on allegations of planting a bomb in the Mombasa-bound bus in which thirteen people died.

However, there was insufficient evidence to convict this political icon without provoking an uprising from Mombasa to Kisumu and from Mt Kilimanjaro to Mt Kenya. Indeed, nothing short of a conspiracy could get rid of this irritant to Jomo Kenyatta and his government for good.

In the words of the chairman of that parliamentary select committee: "government you have heard!" In conclusion, Mr Mwangale, the chairman, narrated a story on the day that he delivered the report to the fully packed parliament, including the public gallery.

"Mr Speaker, sir," he announced, "in our land there is a story told about a hyena that terrorised villagers. Day in, day out the hyena would invade the kraal, attack and run away with goats. The villages then created a vigilante group.

"The villagers went around looking for that hyena but did not find him. But they knew the cave where he lived.

"Standing outside the cave and with one voice, those villagers called out: 'declared Sir, we know that you are in there, and we know that you have heard us, we know that you know your crimes so even if you don't answer…

"Sir, even if you don't answer, even if you don't act; we know that you are the culprit, and that you have heard us."

He then declared, "government, we have done a thorough job; we know how JM was kidnapped and by whom, where he was taken and tortured before being killed."

"We know that inside there where you are, you listening to these calls and that you have heard us," and with that he concluded his submission; a clear indictment of the Jomo Kenyatta government, which by then had perfected the art and science of assassinations.

The arrival of Yusufu at Salimo's district evoked Yusufu's sweet and bitter memories as the doctor for detainees and the friend of the mighty and lowly. It also gave him a chance to remember his close shave with the law. This occasion also gave Salimo a chance to reflect on the many days that they spent sipping coffee and juice that had been paid for by JM himself. It also gave them a chance to recount the many days they lost demonstrating that murder of JM Kariuki; the confrontation between students, the police, the paramilitary wing of the government and the law.

One occasion they could recount when the whole campus was invaded by the police and, as they came to know them, Kamaliza's boys. Kamaliza was the nickname students had given to Jomo Kenyatta. This simply means "the exterminator".

On this occasion, the students were marking the first anniversary of the death of JM. The students pelted motorists on the highway. Uhuru highway was always the battleground. The name Uhuru itself, signifying "independence", was poignant every year when this event was marked. Students carrying boulders would barricade the highway, order motorists to turn around and if they did not obey, the students would smash car windows and windscreens with a hail of stones.

Often, simply, the police would be standing on one side of Uhuru Highway and the students on the other side of the road. There would be mini-skirmishes all day long until out of sheer irritation, tempers would be flying on both sides, causing some student to hurl stones at the police, to which the police would respond with a hail of tear gas and the crack of whips and batons.

This would send a wave of frightened members of the public and that wave would run from Uhuru Highway all the way to River Road and beyond. Some people ran simply because they saw a crowd running from the opposite side. You only found out what was happening when the wave died out in some place distant from the city.

Salimo remembered that on one of these occasions with his friends, they ran on foot for about ten kilometres and spent the night with Salimo's parents.

The news that evening was a tale of terror and mayhem at the campus. The police were charging at and hitting anything on site.

Indeed, on the television news that night, there were tales of all manner of terror, injuries, rape and sheer brutality, as well as arrests. During the next day, Salimo and his friends came to learn that students were chanting "Kamaliza at work!"

The campus newsletter, known as the Platform, that morning ran the news flash: Police Rioting on Campus. The front-page news was nothing but the tales of rioting at the main campus. There was a catalogue of property damage and pictures of gruesome injuries sustained by students during the twelve hours of generalised madness.

This visit also gave Salimo and his colleagues a chance to remember the moment of their graduation a few years ago. As was the tradition, they all congregated at the Legendary Graduation Square, waiting for the pomp and noise caused by the arrival of the legendary Jomo Kenyatta, the University Chancellor, to confer degrees.

Give the devil his due. Jomo Kenyatta was a great orator, a man who knew how to engage with his audience, whether you loved or hated him. On these occasions he would declare, "here on this ground there was great bloodshed; Shujaa Harry Thuku was killed on this ground; we others had to run for our lives".

He would admonish, "Therefore, you young people must not take independence for granted."

"I know that many of you think that, now that we have Uhuru, now we can do anything as we like; some of you like to think that Uhuru means freedom from hard work!"

"That's not true," he announced.

"Indeed, we would like to announce that Uhuru also means hard work."

With that pronouncement, Jomo Kenyatta brought into being the slogan "UHURU na KAZI" meaning freedom and handwork.

He also immediately announced his famous slogan of "Harambee".

Harambee soon became the means to escape from poverty, to escape injustice; or to climb the ladder through the middle class, even to the upper class.

On this occasion, Jomo Kenyatta also warned that you cannot go "around pissing in the middle of the street or Uhuru Highway in the name of our national independence!"

Uwezi kukoja katikati ya barabara huku hujidai eti tuko sasa taifa huru!

The above were Jomo Kenyatta's exact words in Swahili

To emphasise the point, he repeated in English: because we are a free nation, a free people or are independent from the colonialists, that doesn't give you the freedom or the audacity to stand in the middle of the highway or in the street and urinate in public, declaring that you do this in the name of freedom or in the name of independence!

"Hapana!"

"In my view – and this is the position of government – if you do so, or if anybody breaks the law or acts with impunity, you will be arrested and dealt with according to the law of the land," he warned.

Of course after such an event, the public would have occasion to speak all manner praise or ill words towards Jomo Kenyatta. One such rumour narrated how, upon release from detention, the President would be driving from the State House to his Gatundu home. Excited villagers, white and black, would line the street and road to watch the motorcade. He found this offensive. He imagined that some of the white faces were mocking him: "There goes the leader of Mau Mau." This would also remind him of the many days in detention.

He instructed his bosom friend, the Minister for Lands and Settlement to do something about this. No sooner than the concern was raised, all the people living within a few kilometres from the road were relocated to other parts of the country so the President could go home in peace! Soon this gave way to the construction of famous Gatundu Hospital built on the Harambee spirit. The project became legendary as it became the gateway to ascending power. Yusufu remembered leading a delegation of Muslim scholars to pay their homage to the sage or make their sacrifice. Usually the sacrifice was a fat cheque or donation befitting a gift to the Head of State. Such a package or envelope was the passport to higher heights!

Those who exaggerated Jomo Kenyatta's greed for land would recount unproven tales of how this great Kenyan acquired immense wealth within a relatively short span in power.

"Jomo Kenyatta was his own a land surveyor, quantity surveyor and mapping expert all rolled into one," one popular line ran.

The spin doctors usually telling this in pure Swahili would narrate how on one instance after the government had acquired land from the colonial farmers using a loan from the British Government, Jomo Kenyatta one morning instructed his trusted driver and ADC to fill the tank of his beloved Land Rover. Entering the farm, the driver computed the distance the vehicle would drive on the full tank and divided this into four quarters, each representing the four arms of the square. Driving first east, the party then turned south, then west before turning north and finally east to complete the square. All the land mapped out in this manoeuver was declared the Jomo Kenyatta farm. These were those who did not like Jomo Kenyatta.

But for those who found Jomo Kenyatta to be their champion, he was the right man to do business with. He did not represent extreme views, as prevalent elsewhere on the continent. He was a man of peace and prosperity. He understood what was best in life for himself and those around him.

Yusufu would always round up an evening by relating the story of Waruru Kanja, or WK as they called him.

Yusufu would ask Salimo, "Do you remember during the last general election his opponents were using this incident of divorce to try and create a rift between him and his voters?"

"Yes, I do," Salimo answered.

Yusufu continued, "You remember after his opponent had finished speaking after attempting to paint WK pitch black; smearing his name with all manner of mud, but coming to the podium, WK baffled everybody when he announced "brethren we are all each other's keeper, is that not so?"

"Ye-ees" was the resounding cry from the audience. "Let me ask you a question," WK said to the gathering.

"If a brother comes to you and requests to see you for help and assistance in a matter of importance and significance to his life, is it not the requirement of our tribe and our custom to come to his help?" he posed a question.

The response from the crowd was a resounding all in unison, "*Ndiyo, Ndiyo mzee*"! "Yes, yes, it is an obligation!"

Indeed some of them went as far as calling out to "*Toboa!*" meaning "let it out; let the cat out of the bag!"

"Don't hide anything," others shouted back.

WK then narrated the story of how his brother was having difficulty with his wife but did not have a valid reason to tell the court and obtain his wish for divorce. In short, he wanted assistance.

"Now, my brothers and sisters, as your member of parliament, if your brother comes and kneels before you and asks for something, is not the requirement of our custom and practice to give a positive response to this cry for help?"

Indeed the ground was vibrating as if there was a tsunami.

Many of the women were ululating and shouting and saying "that is true, brother" some were raising their skirts in the air and saying "You are our man, a true man!"

***

The one thing that Salimo and other students learned was that medical school is a form of autocracy; an autocracy which was started many years ago and maintained by tradition. There's a pecking order. There's a professor, the lecturer, and everybody else. This tradition transcends the medical profession in general. Indeed, Sagini Mochache summarised the essence of medical school to be, "answer or I shoot". He sketched a frightened little boy in front of the muzzle of a cannon pointing at him in an examination setting saying, "Answer or I shoot". As a group, Salimo and fellow students realised that the only way to beat this system was not to fight it. For that reason, none of them engaged in the student leadership that was extremely radical during that time. Instead, they endeavoured to create an alternative pool of leadership, essentially dedicated to medical school students.

Indeed, Salimo and his fellow students' medical school days can be summarised as an exciting excursion, or learning without any pain.

For example, using their sense of humour, they were able to satirise virtually every event at the medical school to the mutual benefit of all of them. They took every serious or light-hearted situation to be the springboard for organising knowledge and further exploration of information. Each of them collected anecdotal events in his area of study or during the day, which they then shared as a group during the evening when they enjoyed their tea break. They would be eternally grateful to the government and the university who thought it wise to make their life as easy and as simple as possible; they lived in what appeared to be absolute luxury when Salimo and his group looked back at it and examined it later. They enjoyed a five-course dinner. Indeed one could take additional ingredients to keep with them in their room for the ten o'clock tea that they took at 10:00 PM in turns in each of their rooms. In this way, their discussion and study groups and argument groups could continue to the wee hours of the morning, courtesy of the institution that provided the refreshments.

"Joe, do you know what happened today?"

"No," that was Otis introducing an event of the day.

"What happened?" we all asked.

"Joe, that professor of pathology is crazy."

The professor in question was David. David had a good sense of humour and a way of making you learn without any pressure. On this day, he was giving a lecture on rape. To make the point, he asked the class a question but more so addressed one of the ladies who was wearing what one can call a headscarf, indicating that she had some religious leaning. He asked her, "Madam, what would you do if you were in a situation alone out there, attacked, and you understood that whatever you do, rape is inevitable. That you are going to be a victim of sexual assault whether you liked it or not, and you had no way of escaping; what would you do?" The whole class was silent; you could hear a pin dropping.

"Madam, what would you do?" the professor persisted.

The student, embarrassed, replied, "I don't know, maybe I would fight."

"No, no, no, no," interjected the professor with a good expression, using his hands. "What you should do is lie back and relax." With that the whole class broke into a thunderous laughter of excitement.

"Joe, imagine this girl who is so holy – she probably is a virgin – being confronted by this kind of question in itself appears to be sexual assault or harassment. Now she's being advised to lie back and relax."

The professor then went on to explain that the injuries and the damage that is caused by a rapist or a gang rape is essentially the result and the product of resistance from the victim. That's why he advocated that the victim should lie back, relax, shut off

56

their mind to what is happening, and when all the trauma and torture is done, the mind is insulated from the trauma and the body is protected from physical harm.

This small anecdotal story set the students off with many questions; to find out what the definition of rape is, what the dangers or complications of rape are, and in the next meeting it was a wealth of knowledge and experience that the students all gained with each of them going out and seeking information. For example, Joe came with information about infection as a result of rape; what kinds of infections could be transmitted from the rapist and what could be done to prevent disease in the victim. Sagini came with the legal aspects of this case: how is rape managed and handled by the courts. It was clear that when these victims go to the police or the security people, they get discouraged because of the kinds of probing questions and giggling that goes on as they're taking notes; that in itself is an aggravation of the trauma.

It is therefore no wonder that many victims of rape don't report. He even went further to talk about stigma as one of the factors that prevent victims from reporting the rape.

He even went further to inform the group that unfortunately, with rape to some extent, there's a high likelihood that the people who commit rape are people known to the victim; are friends, are relatives; and sometime reporting them causes more problems than enduring the pain. Otis talked about the physical damage that may result and how to diagnose rape and how to give evidence in the case of rape. On and on, the students compiled a dossier of all the elements around rape that would not have been possible to accumulate through the lecture that the professor would be giving next time. Indeed, in the next encounter with the professor, every question he asked about rape, a member of their group was up front answering the questions, to the surprise of the professor.

After a series of sharp and precise answers, the professor stopped and said, "Guys, the five of you– I see you always working together and always laughing, where did you learn about this subject?" he asked. Needless to say, the answer was equally comical.

"From the textbook, sir," they replied.

"I see," the professor responded. "Continue reading those books, you're on the right track; you would make great doctors."

Little did he know that in all they did, it was strategic learning; they were never, never serious students. They adopted strategies that ensured that they learned even more than was expected. On another occasion, it was Otis informing the group of other consternation and confusion that confronted their classmate Maria.

In the medical autocracy, each student is assigned four or five beds in a ward and you take care of any patient who lands in that bed. You must know everything about the patient: the medical history, the social history, and the treatment that these patients are getting. Most importantly, you will lead the team during the ward round, presenting the case, presenting everything that is required, and all in all appearing to be gradually talking at the level of a qualified medical professional. Unfortunately for Maria, the patient she received that day, whom she was presenting to the group, was a patient with priapism. Priapism is a condition where there is a permanent erection. A permanent erection that is painful, painful enough to require the victim to be treated in the hospital. There are many causes, but until this stage as a group saw it as a glorious moment of laughter and entertainment. On the other hand, it formed the basis for a new exploratory encounter with books, friends and professors.

"What happened?" we asked him.

Otis said, "You know, Maria was embarrassed to present this young man who was in severe pain, whose only complaint was that he was unable to suppress penile erection! That his erection was permanent and is unable to bring peace with his muscles. He was suffering from acute 'tendonitis', Otis' terminology for priapism."

Joe then jumped in, "No, no, no, no. Why should that be a problem? In this case he should have been given the opportunity to satisfy as many of his women as possible."

Otis said, "No, no, no, you guys don't understand. This is serious business. A permanent erection beyond a certain moment of time is painful."

"What happened during the presentation?" they asked.

"Maria could only mumble a few words; would not even mention the name of the problem, but eventually she was relieved to learn that this is called penile erection, and on and on until we were told that we need to go and find out what the causes of this condition are." They tried to hazard guesses.

Some of the guesses were simply mischief. For example some said, "Was that his girlfriend? If it was not his girlfriend, it was someone else wife; this is a curse." Others said, "No, the woman must have given him some medication to ensure that she had an exciting day." Others said, "No, what is an erection?" Nobody could explain the mechanism of erection properly.

As a group, once more they went out for a couple of days, to come back with whatever they could learn from journal articles, professors, girls, and colleagues about priapism; what causes it, and how it is treated. In this way, they were now able to explain what an erection is physiologically and anatomically, but not before Otis came with adorable scintillating aspects of an erection. He said, "Guys, my girlfriend was saying the other day when we were having fun that she wanted to see the bone which is inside the organ that makes it stiff." That caused a lot of tumultuous laughter.

Joe responded "No, no, no. In another class you remember Maria was the one who was asking where the bone in the penis is, when we were dissecting the male genitalia. She wanted to see where the bone that makes an erection is."

It was difficult to explain to her that human beings don't have a bone; it is a mechanism of blood, but other animals do have a small bone within the system, or the anatomy of the genitalia. The students were more interested to know the treatment for this odd condition. "No, we were told that you give painkillers like Panadol, and eventually if nothing works, you have to puncture the organs so that you let out the blood and the clots that may have formed in the system, so that flow can be restored"

"Thank God," Otis said, "You don't have to do amputation."

An equally potent system for organising knowledge and learning and retrieving it at an appropriate time was the creation of mnemonics, that let you remember facts, which are too many to accumulate and retrieve on time. So many were these mnemonics created that at some stage one of Salimo's colleagues volunteered to create mnemonics of mnemonics. It worked like this: if you wanted to know all the muscles of the hand, you created a mnemonic. If you wanted to know all the muscles and their functions of the whole upper limb starting from the fingers and the shoulder, then by the time you were able to recall all this, you needed to get mnemonics for the forearm, mnemonics for the mid-arm, mnemonics for the upper arm, and mnemonics for the shoulder. To remember all this you created one mnemonic which was a mnemonic of the mnemonics of the upper limb. It was all exciting but the important thing is that they were all strategies that they invented to enable them to excel in mundane and dead subjects like anatomy.

Little did they know that there was a science to it, an educational foundation to what they were doing based on experimentation. Later on, Salimo learned that there's such a thing as surface learning, deep learning, and strategic learning. Indeed, to a large extent they explored all of them. They explored surface learning; through which they memorised many things and found it to be extremely inefficient. They did deep learning but it was not possible because deep learning is dependent on situations that have a long-term effect, and were being taught sequentially. It's accumulative, so deep learning only would work effectively if you knew what kind of problem you would solve without information. Otherwise all the learning until they reached clinical years was abstract and a pain. Later on when they learned about problem-based learning, case-based learning; all these kinds of new developments in learning, they understood that they were on to something great.

Coming back to the subject of rape, the professor of forensic pathology asked, "Who can tell me… Who can define for us rape? The definition of rape." There were many answers, but probably the one which stuck out until later in life in Salimo's mind was the one from Obush. Obush was one of the earlier ones who raised their hands, but since he was full of mischief, he would normally wait until "information had been exhausted", as he termed it, and then he would crown it all with his own two cents. "Yes, what is rape, Obush?"

"Sir, rape is crash-landing in Thighland."

"What?" the professor asked.

"Yes, rape is crash-landing in Thighland."

Even before the gales of laughter had settled down – the professor was equally tickled – he asked, "What do you mean by crash-landing in Thighland?"

"Sir, it means taking the goods without invitation. It is a form of breaking in, so since these goods are in between the thighs, so it is crash-landing in Thighland."

Of course this was not the medical answer the professor was expecting but it had all the raw elements of rape. For example, there are the elements of consent, elements of no negotiation, and the fact that one had to define rape in precise terms to include penetration and collect evidence, and what amount of evidence would convince even the most negative judge or police officer that indeed rape had taken place. That there was no negotiation, that the victim was ambushed, and the victim did resist and that actually there was evidence within the canal – the genitalia of the victim, that there had been full penetration. Indeed for this group, as they call themselves, they used every opportunity, ridiculous, hurtful, enjoyable, whatever the occasion, to ensure that they accumulated the necessary body of scientific knowledge that would see them through the medical school.

Soon thereafter, as a group they started what they called a newsletter that was always published on the school chalkboard. Every morning before class there would be a news item that was posted. These were the days before there was WhatsApp or Twitter, they were days when the students used the most rudimentary means of communication. There was no cell phone, there was no easy access to the telephone, so everything was only shared by printing it on the board. Every medical student soon learns that medical school, though demanding, allows for a multitude of opportunities to develop individualised coping mechanisms. But even more effective is a combination of the methodologies that are cumulative or pooled from groups of students. These pooled or group mechanisms, probably work much in the same manner that herd immunity operates to protect groups from contracting diseases. No wonder that problem-based learning, which is based on small group tutorial approach as opposed to the cathedral lectures style, is considered to be highly successful.

Salimo and his 'Joe' group, as they called themselves, was a closely knit social and study group with group norms and practices. This persisted well into postgraduate training. Like any social grouping, the members naturally looked into each other's interest. However no member was immune to being victim of some mischief or naughty games.

Gradually they had started to like medicine. It became exciting and a lifelong calling. How did this become a reality? How did they transform?

Looking back, Salimo believes it was a result of a coincidence: a meeting of good friends, all from different backgrounds and from different ethnic groups, but sharing some common beliefs, and what they would come to term 'galaxies'. Galaxies meant that there were different areas of interest for each of the members of the group. But, at some stage these interests did collide or did intersect at different points of the fields of interaction. For example, Salimo and James held very strong beliefs of and were enamoured of radicalism. They saw things in black and white. Whereas Otis and Sagini were of a common breed in that they loved members of the opposite sex. As for Joe, he loved diplomacy. There's nothing he could not leverage out of the system, given time. Indeed, from time to time all members of the team needed to be resurrected or redeemed from certain transgressions.

In this instance, the other four would turn to Joe to pull the strings or smoothen things. But, to Salimo the most important thing that happened was that they shared a common sense of humour. They were able to cultivate some mutual respect for each other. They were able to take most things with a pinch of salt.

***

Examination was another ball game, different from teaching and learning, as Sagini put it. Examination is life in Africa. According to Sagini, examination in medicine is like an African tropical forest. What did he mean? In examination, you can expect anything, like when in the forest, at any moment some animal can leap out of the thickets. You never know whether it's a snake, whether it's a leopard, or whether it's a lion; from the African tropical forest you should expect any animal at any time. For example, Bundi Jared, on occasion of surgery, was confronted with a most peculiar, strange-looking lesion afflicting the scrotum of a middle-aged man.

This is the first time he was seeing a melanoma, or a cancer of the skin, affecting the scrotum skin. Normally melanomas are in the exposed parts of the body; easy to diagnose, easy to see. But in this case this melanoma affected the scrotum. It was the blackest scrotum Bundi had ever seen. For him the saviour in this exam was the history he obtained and the thorough examination he carried out, but when it came to determining what this ghastly lesion was, he was entirely baffled. It did not help matters when the examiner, Ambrose, confronted him and asked him the first question.

"Doctor Bundi..." normally the medical doctors will mix a bit of mischief and ridicule in order to mess with the poor victim, the student. Whenever you hear the examiner starting with "Doctor, tell us," you know that you are in for a rough time.

"Yes, Doctor. Have you ever seen this condition before?" enquired the examiner.

"No sir, never in my life as a medical student," replied Bundi.

"Unfortunately this is the most unfortunate condition at which to encounter this strange condition," replied Ambrose with laughter that sent Mr Wambowa laughing his head off, raising his leg and throwing his hands in the air.

"Doctor, you said you have never seen this condition?"

"Yes sir."

"Please then tell us about this condition, what do you make of it?"

Then Bundi, to his credit, gave them everything they needed to know about how to examine a mass, and how to you elicit science and symptoms. According to his differential diagnosis, the most probable conditions was terrible because he could not make head or tail of this condition, and all he could diagnose was that it was most likely a cancer and he could not bring himself to conclude that it was the cancer of the skin. He could not... the physical examination would not enable him to determine whether this mass was from the testis or from the skin.

Indeed, after a brief consultation between the two examiners, they agreed that the student did a good job despite the fact that he could not conclude conclusively what the condition was. That in itself did not constitute a major failure for a final year medical student.

"What would you do under these conditions?" was the next set of questions leading into the treatment, management and eventual prognosis.

"I'll take a biopsy," he responded.

"Of what?" was the question from Ambrose.

"The mass."

"Which mass is this?"

Ambrose was the kind of person who would want you be precise in the use of medical terminology and be upset if instead of saying, "We'll do a laparotomy or open the abdomen," the student stated, "We will go in and check what's happening".

If you said that, you would be in for a rough time. He would laugh in the most sarcastic manner and say, "Doctor, you don't go in a patient." Anytime you wound a patient you will be accused of grievous bodily harm. This injury is trauma you will be causing if you wound a patient. He would say, "We will open the abdomen and examine."

By the time Bundi left this most unwelcome incident he was convinced that he would have to retake the examination. This opinion was based on the way the examiners were laughing, and the way the mass did not seem to be anything he could recognise.

The fact that he could not determine whether it was from the skin, soft tissue, or the testis, for him was enough evidence that he had failed. It was therefore for him a great surprise when he was told that he had passed. Indeed, these final examinations were a sense of great frustration and torture to the students, particularly when they were not well prepared. Indeed, Olila Wafula, or Omwami our comrade as they called him, on the day the results were pinned out and he saw his name on the list, he could not believe it. He asked his colleague to check again whether his number and his name were on there.

When the colleague confirmed that indeed he had passed, Olila went away for easily eight hours and drank himself silly. When he reappeared at dinnertime, he made everybody remain silent for a moment, then he announced, "Friends, I know all of you were afraid, were praying for me. Some of you had concluded that I would fail, but let me tell you that God is great. I passed my examination."

Indeed, his compatriot, his close friend, took the occasion also to announce that at exactly 9:00 PM he would be holding a ceremony to which he was inviting everybody. He would be marking the end of education and learning in his life.

"What will you do?" they asked.

"Don't worry," he said, "please come to Kilometer 101."

Kilometer 101 was a popular spot near the hostels, with a nice stack of chairs, where a student would sit after lunch and before dinner and exchange trivialities and laugh about life in general. Indeed, at 9 o'clock there was a bonfire outside and to the great consternation of everybody, the newly crowned Dr Were had set all his textbooks on fire. He announced, "Gentlemen, it was a grave mistake for me to register as a medical student. Luckily I made it. I have enough knowledge and skills to live on for the rest of my life."

"I have no intention of continuing the torture by retaining these text books," he continued. Little did he know that education can be defined as what remains when you have burnt all your textbooks, what you retained as a result of working through the huge textbooks. What you retained in you can be defined as education.

***

Salimo had said before that their group avoided student leadership at the higher level, but that didn't mean they didn't have friends who were in the power game of the university.

Once, Salimo had a colleague that he and his group members interacted with from time to time, who was called Sebastiano Ooga Keragita. His surname signifies the arrival of tractors in the village.

Sebastiano enjoyed playing the power game. Not that he had any leadership skills, but he enjoyed advocating for others; pressing their cases, pushing management to the brink.

Indeed, he was one of the firebrands fighting for a flyover across Uhuru highway where it intersected the campus of the university. He was a feverish fighter for another flyover across Nyerere Avenue where the Avenue had divided the halls of residence, but intersected the halls of residence.

The Uhuru highway flyover was a source of recurrent and violent confrontations between the police and the students and usually, the public was worst off.

From time to time, students, especially just before exams, would be mobilised and put rocks, burning tyres and far more obstacles and block off Uhuru Highway. Uhuru Highway was the major artery transecting the city of Nairobi and connecting the country from coast to lake.

So any major disruption of traffic on that road would be felt from Mombasa by the Indian Ocean, to Lake Victoria. The wheels separated all the way, 500 kilometres in either direction.

Indeed, eventually, the government did give in, but not before putting up a stiff fight in parliament. The firebrand, Mulu Mutisya, an illiterate Member of Parliament, courtesy of Jomo Kenyatta, argued virulently against the spoiled brats; the students who were demanding more and more.

He would say, "Even chicken can walk across Uhuru Highway. Why can't these elite walk across Uhuru Highway?"

He would say, "They are asking for dialogue." On another page, he wondered, "This dialogue," as he called it, "if it is food, give them the dialogue, let them eat. Why do you deny them dialogue?" Indeed, on another occasion, when the issue was boiling over, it was his stand to rail at Karl Marx. He said, "This Karl Marx, where is he? Bring him here. Why is the government afraid to arrest Karl Marx who is the one causing our students to riot? This is a terrorist who should be arrested," amid great laughter in parliament.

So fierce was the war that Sebastiano unleashed on the management that at the first instance he was expelled from the halls of residence.

No wonder when the Vice Chancellor met him the next time, he was a leading member of the SRC, a student representative council demanding for better conditions at the hostel, demanding that the underpass to be constructed should be manned by security during certain hours because now a new problem had arisen. Two problems had arisen actually. One, students were being mocked on Uhuru Highway as they went through the tunnel.

Secondly, during the rainy season, the tunnel would be flooded with water. The same fate would befall the tunnel joining the two halls of residence.

Indeed, the straw which broke the camel's back in the case of Sebastiano, forcing the university to expel him, was when he was arrested with a hammer and axe, trying to knock down the embankment that was erected to prevent students from walking across the road, forcing them to go through the tunnel.

The university could not take this anymore, so he was expelled from the university for good.

Many of them never heard of him again, only for him to re-emerge during Moi's time. By this time, he had graduated from the University of Dar es Salaam with a degree in Economics.

He was walking with the coffee bot of Kenya.

As soon as Moi came into power, he needed people with strong views, people who were not tainted with corruption, to clean up the coffee market.

During Kenyatta's time, coffee smuggling from Uganda was legalised, so to say. "Indeed, in Sebastiano's world, you must always be on the move." That was his favourite statement. He said, "If you stay stationary, you risk failure in life." At least that's how he explained his resurrection through University of Dar es Salaam: "You will fall from the sky like a plane which stalls, and that was the effect of inertia."

He advocated that you must always be on the move, looking for opportunities here and there. For once, he could prove that by moving around, he had taken advantage of the opportunity that the University of Dar es Salaam offered to radical students of its university.

Now, in Jomo Kenyatta's last days, Amin had ascended power in Uganda. Everything had broken down. The market of coffee had broken down and the Kenyans were doing roaring business at Chepkube, which was the major entry point of Ugandan coffee into the Kenyan market.

Indeed, during one of these years, for the first time, Kenya recorded an unprecedented positive balance of payments, thanks to the booming coffee business between Uganda and Kenya.

It is said that once following allegations not supported by any evidence, when culprits were taken to Jomo Kenyatta and the issue was brought to his cabinet, with the plea to release more funds to curb smuggling of coffee from Uganda, he asked the following questions in response. "Attorney General, what these people doing here? Are these Kenyans buying the coffee from Uganda with their money?"

"Yes, sir," responded the Attorney General.

"Are they stealing the coffee?" thundered Jomo Kenyatta.

"No, sir," replied the visibly shaken Attorney General.

"Are they robbing anybody?" Jomo Kenyatta demanded to know.

"No, sir," replied the Attorney General.

"They pay for the coffee," Jomo Kenyatta continued with the interrogation.

"Yes. Yes, Mr President," the Attorney General answered.

"So what is the problem?" the President asked.

"Sir, but this is smuggling, and it is affecting the economy," the Attorney General tried to counter the logic of his boss.

"Are Kenyans getting rich?" asked the President.

"Yes, sir," answered the Attorney General.

Jomo Kenyatta wondered aloud, "What's wrong with you guys? What's wrong with the process?" The President said that the Cabinet would not devote any more money to stop Kenyans from getting rich. That was the end of the matter.

When Moi came in, he thought it was to earn a few points on the power game because he had declared a passing cloud. Moi wanted to prove a point.

Corruption was number one on the list of the crimes that needed to be fought. Indeed, Moi added corruption to the three sworn enemies of Kenya: the first being ignorance, the next being poverty, and the next being deceit. He added corruption to the four mortal enemies of the country.

So Sebastiano was a natural candidate because he was already working for the coffee board which was in charge of a huge coffee store. He was in charge of that warehouse.

Moi appointed him as a special czar on the coffee business and that's how he called himself the Coffee Czar, having learned something about the czar of Russia.

He was the only one that would issue permits for anybody to deliver coffee into the warehouse.

The warehouse was the only outlet of Kenyan coffee in the international market. He opened his office closet to get good water to ensure that all the coffee which was coming from that root had those necessary papers.

Many of the cronies of Jomo Kenyatta would come with him with fictitious letters from Moi indicating that they had been allowed to deliver coffee into the warehouse.

Sebastiano was not to be fooled.

Indeed, he instructed his secretary that he will not see anybody or he will not read any letter that was not signed in ink: green ink, fresh, no copy. Of course green ink was the ink which Moi used to sign.

He would only see people, only read letters which not only were signed in green pen; not in a ballpoint pen, but in a green ink pen and the ink had to be fresh.

So after a year of this tough talk, the smuggling of coffee eventually ran its course. Indeed, Amin was also driven out of power and as a consequence, the marketing of coffee in Uganda resumed through the right channels. Although it was being exported through the port of Mombasa, it had the correct papers from the point of origin in Uganda. It was not happening through the middlemen.

But this was not before Sebastiano rose to the even higher level of the "anti-coffee-smuggling czar"!

Now that he was in the limelight, he was a very popular young man.

He bought himself ten hectares of coffee and tea, in a neighbouring district.

He would visit this place from time to time in the company usually of a different companion whom he described as his new wife.

Every wife who passed through to go and see this tea was allocated two hectares.

During the lifetime of Sebastiano's stint as the chairman of the coffee board, he allocated 20 or so hectares of this coffee and this form of tea to every new girlfriend that came his way.

This happened until Salimo and friends reminded Sebastiano that he had exceeded the ten hectares that he owned by another ten, therefore soon he may have to subdivide that land to half hectares to accommodate all the beneficiaries that he had brought through.

Sebastiano continued thereafter to plunge himself into actual politics, seeking to be elected into Parliament; and he would have done so if it was not for the corrupt ways that the elections were being held during his time. At this stage, Moi had decreed that the sacred board could be manipulated.

Therefore, he had instructed Parliament to change the mode of voting to that from secret ballot to lining behind the candidates of their agents at the polling stations.

In this way, Moi had argued, there was absolute transparency and accountability during their voting process.

He even added another element to this, that there would be no reason for a parliamentary candidate to be given a separate ticket to one campaign. Therefore, there would be one day when all candidates or contestants would address programmed public rallies in the constituency.

In other words, those managing the electoral process would draw up a program of public rallies across the constituency and individuals who were contesting would present themselves on that day and each would be given an hour or so to address the crowd. In Moi's words, this gave the public the opportunity to first-hand assessment of the candidates.

In his view, there would be no cheating.

Little did he know that impunity is stronger than any fraudulent means that you make to influence an election.

On this occasion, the electoral office would count. Once they knew who the preferred candidate by Moi was, they would do everything to lie.

For example, they would count single individuals singly for their candidate who was preferred and then to make the others lose, they would count every fifth person as a person. Since there were no record of the lines and the queues, nobody with amount of complaints, even going back to court, would find evidence to show that it was unfair, that Moi won through unfair means. They would simply go by the numbers that the electoral office had presented to the court.

This was one of the darkest moments of the electoral process in Kenya.

Indeed, it generally worked against individuals like Sebastiano who might cause trouble to the Moi government, who had become too transparent.

In other words, Moi had gone full circle from being a fighter against corruption to the prophet of corruption. He was the high priest of corruption during his tenure as President.

Sebastiano was one of those firebrand student leaders who fought against what he considered an unqualified Vice Chancellor. This Vice Chancellor had been a close ally of Jomo Kenyatta, before he was appointed ambassador to St James Court, which was considered in Kenyans' view, the highest office you can occupy. When it came to appointing a new Vice Chancellor, Jomo Kenyatta started to appoint this son of the soil as the new Vice Chancellor.

He had never been elected at the university. He never held any position at the university. His main qualification was that he was a close and trusted ally, of Jomo Kenyatta.

The students did not miss the notice that he loved playing golf.

Indeed, every time there was a crisis at the university – and this was an annual event – he would be missing during the Senate meetings and it would be chaired by the deputy Vice Chancellor.

A student would then conclude that he was out playing golf.

Indeed, golf became the face of leisurely pastimes for the rich; what the students considered as bourgeois, and it was to be fought.

No wonder many of them never took a liking to golf.

Golf was equivalent to a life of luxury, a life out of ill-gotten goods.

***

"What is wrong with our friend, Joe?" Terry confronted the group.

"Why do you ask?" the three impulsively probed, expecting to hear more as their appetite for a juicy banter had been provoked!

That evening at the discotheque, it was four group members. Sibuor, or Joe as he was commonly known, was not there, but there was Terry, Otis, Salimo and Sagini. They were still waiting for Sibuor to arrive.

With great excitement, Terry proceeded to narrate from the grapevine.

"What is it, Joe, that you have heard about our friend?" They wanted to hear more.

"No, don't worry, it's just a big story about Joe's new find," Terry responded.

It so happens that at this stage, Joe had got what he considered a perfect match. He referred to her as his future soulmate. Joe described her as a real thoroughbred, of right pedigree, a mix between a Masaii and some other tribe.

The lady was slim, tall, with a long neck. She was close to the height of Joe himself. Every time they went out, Joe would not forget to tell us how gracefully she walked, how wonderful she was. "This is my kind of woman."

Just as Terry was about to delve into the gossip about the rare beauty, on this occasion they had a new arrival into the group, a fellow student, Usman.

Usman, sensing the mood, lost no time in adding spice to the story.

"The best, the most beautiful women, I've found in Somaliland. They're amazing," he said. "You can't find another one or another group that is consistently, in big numbers, looking glamorous and beautiful," Usman added for emphasis.

But Usman's storyline collapsed amidst resonating laughter from the group, when he announced that actually his girlfriend was also from Somaliland!

Anyway, Terry then informed the group that it would appear that Joe idolised this "new find", as he called her. He would take her out regularly, as was the tradition amongst them, that you treated your future spouse carefully and gave her the best attention. He would take her out, barely give her a smooch on the cheek, and drop her at the women's hostels.

"This is where the trouble is," Terry said.

"What do you mean, 'the trouble'?" the group asked.

"The trouble is that the lady's expecting more. Every time they go out, and it's now not once, not twice; it's several times. Every time they go out, Joe just brings her back home, treats her like some kind of puppy, and lets her escape into the sanctuary of her room. This is not going well with the lady. Indeed, she has nicknamed Joe her paediatric." At this stage, Joe was doing his postgraduate in Paediatrics, and the analogy the lady was making was that he still had to go through the age of childhood to adolescence before he could become a real man, a man who knows what a woman wants.

In other words, Joe was not rising to the occasion or demonstrating virility or that he was a man, by the definition of this babe who considered herself "full-blooded" and this is how Terry described her; someone who expected more than just a smooch on the cheek.

"No, no, no, no, a woman always requires action, action, action," Sagini added.

"And that is the problem, gentlemen," Terry lamented, "Joe is letting our team down. He's making it appear that all of us are amateurs when it comes to women. No, no, no, Joe must be told that he needs to prove himself," Terry concluded in absolute disappointment.

As if by design, Joe appeared from nowhere, always beaming with a smile. "Hi, Joe, you came at the right time, welcome!" they called him in a chorus.

Unfortunately, they all were too excited to read how, or to imagine how, he would take this news. So immediately as he arrived, Terry blurted out, "Joe, what's wrong with you?"

"What do you mean, what's wrong with me?" Joe enquired.

"No, Joe, you are letting us down," Terry continued.

"Who are 'we' and how am I letting us down?"

"Joe, you are letting the Joe group down."

"What do you mean?" still Joe persisted. They then allowed Otis to narrate the story.

"Joe, in the grapevine, you are known as the Paediatric. Your new-found love? In her assessment, you are no more than pre-adolescent."

"What do you mean, I'm not adolescent?" Joe asked, with a tinge of irritation.

"The lady says you can't perform."

"What do you mean I can't perform?" Joe asked.

"Yes, she says you treat her like she's not even a teenager. That you don't even go beyond just a smooch on the cheek," Terry explained.

"Joe, tell us, since you met her, have you had sex with her?" Joe answered, "No."

Then all of them burst out laughing. "Why?" they asked in a chorus.

Then Joe went on to tell them, "You guys, you don't understand."

"What do you think we don't understand? We don't understand women?" Terry wondered aloud.

"No. This woman…" Joe continued, "is my dream wife. I'm not going to mess with her at this stage. I'm going to prepare her for the right moment. Yes, this is my idol. She's my princess. I'm going to respect her; I'm going to treat her like a wife."

Then Terry jumped into it. He said, "That is the trouble with you, Joe. Have you lost your knack for women?"

"Joe, this woman is going around and slandering you and saying you've got no fire. You are like a gun that is used for sports."

At this moment in time, Joe was really getting worked up and irritated. Then they posed the question, "Joe, what are you going to do about it?"

"I'm not going to have anything to do with this woman," Joe responded. "I made a mistake; I don't want to see her!" Joe was livid with anger.

"This is not my kind of woman," Joe continued. "A woman with that kind of thinking and mentality; no, is not worth being my wife."

Terry jumped in, "No, no, no, no, Joe, that would not help things."

"What do you mean it would not help things?" Joe retorted.

Terry then explained to him, "In this kind of circumstance, you must go and prove yourself. You must go and prove that you are a man. That's what you must and should do. Otherwise, the whole Joe group is doomed. We are classified as duds."

"No, I'm never, ever, going to take this woman out." Joe was emphatic.

Then Otis could not restrain himself and jumped into the fray.

"No, no, no Joe. If I were you, this is what I would do if I were you."

"What would you do?" Joe retorted.

"I would go to a blacksmith. I'd get anything that would make me really sharp, fiery, a real warrior. I'd then go back to this woman, and the damage I'd do. It'd require a team of highly skilled gynaecologists to put her together."

"No, no way am I going to go to this woman," Joe angrily responded, indicating that he did not want to continue to be part of this discussion.

"Joe, how will you achieve this?" they all wanted more insight from Otis.

"I will try everything in the book," Otis explained, "including hot massage or this new thing, Viagra." At that stage Viagra was coming into the picture.

"I will even try Viagra!" just to prove a point, he said, "Sure, I'll go with a vengeance. I'll ensure that the good name of Joe is restored."

Needless to say, their compatriot Joe was not convinced, or at least that's what he told them. As this was an occasion to be jubilant and to relax, neither Joe nor the group were going to be let down by a moment of indiscretion from one of their members. Now that they had a completely new troop of ladies accompanying them, and were soon arriving, they decided to let the matter lay to rest, to allow Joe some time to reflect over this matter, and come with a convincing response.

Bowing out of the race was no option in their view. They knew Joe as the man who led the troops. Indeed, on a previous occasion, he had been accused of being too dramatic and too agile, in his room which was next to door to Usman's. Whenever his exciting girlfriend arrived, Usman had to migrate to another room.

"What do you mean, you had to migrate?" they asked him on one of these evenings when they were enjoying their usual coffee break in one of the Joe's rooms.

"When the lady arrives, this lady…this exciting lady he has found from the neighbouring hospital, the nurse…when she arrives in Joe's room there is like an earthquake in motion!" Usman lamented. "Things are falling all over; noises are heard from the room. I couldn't sleep, gentlemen."

They then had appointed one of them to be the judge, to find out whether this is something which needs to be condemned, or it is something to be condoned. Joe then confessed that, yes, he was not being accused wrongly, but it was not that dramatic, it was not that noisy.

"No, no, no," Osman protested, "It is worse than that. Remember last time I had to come and pound on your door, boom, boom, boom, boom, to tell you to tone it down." At that stage they were all breaking down with laughter.

Indeed on the occasion when they were being told about this issue, Jalang'o was also there. He explained, "No, no, no, no, this Joe is a bad man."

"Why?" they all wanted to know.

He said, "You know, I'm the one who discovered this girl, the nurse, from the hospital. I took Joe to go and take a look and tell me whether my assessment, that this was a real angel, was misplaced. The next thing I knew, Joe was dating her, and she was frequently in his room which was directly below my room. But I understood and I didn't raise a complaint or any protest."

They then asked why.

"Because I understood that Joe is more handsome than I am," Jalang'o continued. Jalang'o then continued to narrate this painful encounter, stating that the lady would have had no problem with who to choose between Joe and himself. There was no match; no competition between him and Joe, so he let it to go.

"Little did I know that I lost a real woman," Jalang'o concluded, amidst seismic laughter from all of them, including him.

Anyway, now that the matter of the new-found girl was temporarily laid to rest, they had time to concentrate on the business of the night, to enjoy themselves.

***

Olila is the one who came up with the triple prophylactic therapy.

The deal was that if half a night before sexual encounter, you swallowed eight capsules of the tetracycline and you swallowed two tablets of Flagyll, you ran your quota for protection against any venereal disease. The Flagyll took care of flagellates and the tetracycline took care of all the bacterial infections.

To be completely covered, you needed to deal with the external parasites, mainly of the fungal origin. Therefore, he recommended a total spray of all the genitalia of some insecticide. Obviously, all of these things had to be done in moderation, and there is a history – or at least a recorded case – of fatality poisoning using pyrethrum bases as the external fumigant against the parasites.

Nevertheless, on Friday when the medical schools received their boom, which was a kind of allowance which was given by the State to the students once a month, Olila would not go back to the hostel that day. The School of Medicine was usually the last to receive their boom. Therefore, Olila would be swallowing these capsules of the tetracycline and swallowing Flagyll. By the end of the queue, he would have taken the full dose of these items. Not that they were nice and pleasant to take, but their medical effect was more beneficial to the individual than taste. So Olila would handle anatomy books from the dissection, get his boom, and disappear into the city. Inevitably, he would re-emerge in a popular spot called Matunda.

At Matunda, the toilet girls converged on Saturdays, for they knew that there was potential to catch fat fish.

For them, as students, or the ENNOS Group as they called themselves, they did not stop at poking fun at each other and the other students. They even extended further to their lecturers and professors. For example, they nicknamed Nelson 'De Pesa'.

'De Pesa' because there is in urology, a catheter for living urethral retention called the De Pesa Catheter.

Being a urologist, he taught them about the use of this De Pesa catheter. Unknown to him, it was noted that whenever he came to the theatre for the operation, he would approach with it hung around his neck and it would drop all the monies that he carried.

This was before the day of the soft money. The day of Thomas Cook's Traveller's Cheques. It was before the day of the credit card so the only way you were fully financially covered was if you carried sufficient notes in your pocket.

And so the moment they saw him carrying this money around his neck, they immediately called him 'De Pesa'. Pesa in Swahili means money.

Nelson was a likeable professor, liked by the students primarily because he would teach generally. You could be operating in the theatre, and they would be spinning stories at the same time.

He would ask, for example, "Why does Nyerere call Kenya the man-eat-man society?"

The one and only student that answered said, "Sir, it is because of people like you who walk with their money at their neck."

He did not take offense. He was very tickled for the rest of the operation. "So you say I'm a man-eat-man," he said.

Then the student said, "Yes you are a man-eat-man society. That's what they mean by saying that few people have the money and the rest are just struggling."

Nelson acknowledged the analogy and concluded that students were right in their economic analysis.

"But students, you know the only time I have is to make money. I do not have the time to spend it."

Indeed, Nelson's day started at 4 AM and it did not end until midnight. It started with the ward round in one of the private hospitals which ended maybe by 8 AM. He would briefly make an appearance at his department or office at the university.

He would maybe stop in the lecture theatre for 30 minutes. 30 minutes was the standard lecture that he would give and when you left this lecture, you were unlikely to forget it. It was extremely well synthesised with enough hooks upon which you could hang everything that he said and retrieve it at the appropriate time.

Indeed, whenever you met him in the oral examination or the objective structure examination, you would know that you would pass.

De Pesa was the kind of examiner that would ask you what the five causes of urinary retention are.

And once you mentioned one or two, then he would say, "And of course what about this one?" Normally the answer would be yes. He would form his questions in a way that inevitably if you said yes, you stood a 99% chance of getting it right.

Naturally, De Pesa was a popular professor with students.

Indeed, he lived the same life when Salimo was doing an internship under him. De Pesa was the kind of person that would say, "Doc, please start with cauterizing the patient. I'm on the way." Normally, the procedure would end before he arrived. He had great confidence in his students as future interns and as future medical officers.

Under him, many people learned the tricks and their way around the planting business, as he called it. "Doc," he would ask Salimo, "You're saying that these days, you need collateral to buy a car?"

Salimo would say, "Yes sir."

"Oh, things have changed. In my time," he would announce, "All you needed to do was to get your pay slip and go to the bank. Once they saw that you were doctor, they would approve your loan without any collateral."

"Times have changed."

He would continue indicating that he was not totally happy with the decay of the generation of the conditions in the country.

"You know," one day he was telling the students, "If you want to know anything about the politics of this nation, talk to the petrol pump attendants at the Petro station."

"Those people know more than even the newspapers, even the politicians themselves."

Paradoxically, the demise of Nelson commenced at a petrol attendant's station.

It was reported that the attendant noted that he was having a convulsion soon after he filled his tank.

By the time they released him from the seatbelt, he had fractured both hips and both necks of the femur.

This convulsion, which was never explained, led on to one complication after the other to his premature demise at the age of less than 50.

But one can say this is the man who epitomised what is good in medicine. He also epitomised what's good in the relations between a student and a professor.

Each student had the kind of professor that would tickle and make fun of them without creating lifelong enemy and offense.

For example, Salimo found great relief in interacting with De Pesa.

De Pesa trusted him. De Pesa never took offense. "Salimo, do you know that the time we will take here doing this procedure – one hour, by the end of that period, the House of Manji will have made a million sweets and that would have amounted to no less than $100,000 US dollars. For us, we'll earn maybe 20,000 Kenyan shillings. That's $100 per day."

"You know, my son came to… Last week my son asked me to sponsor him for a charity walk. That's when it hit me, that we doctors now are very poorly paid."

"Do you know," he continued, "That when I looked at the diary of my son, already the Chief Secretary had sponsored him for $500 Kenyan shillings a kilometre. When I looked at it, I didn't even want to put my offer on this diary because previously I had only put $5 per kilometre, 5 shillings per kilometre. Oh," he concluded, "We doctors must change. We must find other ways of making money."

For Rafael Makotsi, he found pleasure in teasing Lady Macmillan. Lady Macmillan was a lady from the United Kingdom, as he called it. She was from the UK, not from England as the students tended to say. When there was an occasion to teach and make sure to deliver a lasting impression, she would volunteer herself as the patient for the simulation.

On one such occasion, she intimated that because it takes too long to dilate the pupil of a black man or a woman, she would be the patient the students would all examine. When they want to see the back of the eye, also known as the fundus on the eye, as she explained, because of the pigment, the pupil of the Caucasian or the English people, is already dilated. It doesn't require any medication.

On one of these days, they were on queue to examine the fundus of their lab professor.

"Who will be the first?" she asked.

"Me," immediately Rafael announced.

"Good. Come here. Take this scope and examine my fundus and tell me what you see." They were all curious to see what Rafael would find.

Rafael took much longer than one would expect when you are examining the eye, until Lady Macmillan asked him to tell the other students what he could see.

"Rafael, I think you have had enough time to examine my fundus. What can you see?"

With some consternation, Rafael announced, "Dear Professor Macmillan, this is the most beautiful fundus that I've ever seen in my life."

With that, he set into motion a seismic wave of laughter; even the sickest patient stood up to check what was going on.

"What does that mean, Rafael?"

He then said, "No, madam, it is the most beautiful fundus."

"Does it mean it is normal? What did you see? Did you see any vessels?"

"I saw that it was nice and orange and there was even a small little bulb behind there. I was able to see what looked like normal arteries in the fundus."

"Good," was the confirmation from Lady Macmillan, taking no offense. Obviously, many of the responses from Rafael were sexist. No wonder, the next day, in a clinical bedside session, he was given an X-ray and he would usually be the first one to have a go at examining and telling the other students what he saw, which by the way is a good way of learning by students.

"Okay, Rafael. Tell us what you see." Once more, Rafael was philosophical. He examined it intimately and through all angles, taking it off the machine and looking through the window.

"What did you find, Rafael?" Lady Macmillan asked.

"Oh madam, this is the X-ray of a woman."

With that, once more, there was a reverberation of laughter down the hall. Not that the answer was wrong, but that was not what was expected of him at this stage.

Rather than be upset, Lady Macmillan asked, "And how do you say that it is a woman?"

"Don't you see those two little dots? Those are the nipples," he announced. That set into motion even more laughter. Of course he was right. You could see the nipples which other students might have mistaken for some seedlings, or some seeds, as they call malignancies in the lung.

Then after everything else, he went on to explain that there was nothing wrong with the chest X-ray. It was absolutely normal for a woman.

This kind of exposition, this kind of encounter during clinical teaching formed the thesis of their group of ENNOS. They took this, the light-hearted learning and mixed it with the hard silence and it ensured that they would remember everything about the event and the condition.

Of course there was their beloved Professor Muhanji and Professor Nnochiri. One was a psychiatrist and the other a microbiologist.

Their Professor of psychiatry for the first time enabled them to see psychiatry as a science. Prior to this, all the other teachers made it look like magic. Their definition of a psychotic patient was one that was running naked in the streets and causing havoc.

Muhanji, who was a hard-core member of UPC in Uganda would tell them that psychiatry is a science. You must know your neurology and neuropsychiatry before you can do psychiatry. For him, psychiatry was the hallmark of medicine because that's where intellect was most called for. Anything else, in this hierarchy of science, was lower. Surgery was the lowest of the specialisations because it was essentially highly manual. It was no different than what a butcher does.

But psychiatry required deep understanding of processes and phenomena and a deep knowledge of neuroscience or neurology before you could effectively award someone with the degree.

On the one hand, he tried to influence Salimo – who had marked surgery as his area of future specialisation – to deviate and go to psychiatry.

He announced, "You are far too intelligent to devote all your life in simply cutting."

"Better you join the club of the elite," which is what he called psychiatry.

They were not surprised, therefore, when the students learned that doing his legitimate work of advancing democracy, during the second Obote's ascendency to power, he was shot dead by soldiers manning a roadblock. Naturally, you would imagine that he would be trying to talk them out of the situation and he would not usually be polite.

He would normally say "these therefore" as he pulled up his trouser, to adjust it to the waist, and then he would go on with a really good story about what was about to happen.

Naturally, the soldier saw insolence and would not find whatever he said to them amusing; probably that the time of dictatorship was up! They would find it arrogant and nobody knows if his normally free-flowing sarcastic remarks were what led to his demise.

As for the microbiologist, he was the most of the many good professors that they had come across. He was one of those who were highly cynical about non-evidence based practice of medicine.

On one occasion, he angered all of specialist positions when he announced, "Ladies and gentlemen, today I will be exposing the lingering clinicians who, among other things, have done almost 50-metre-long ECGs for a patient with anxiety. The patient did not really have anxiety."

"They didn't take a good history because the condition they were supposed to be exploring is a condition of anxiety rather than organic pathology. One track mind!" he quipped. "There was no organic pathology with the heart," he lamented.

Indeed, telling the students and impressing them about vaccination, he told a story of this King who had a beautiful daughter. He didn't want her to have any mark on her body, at least the exposed parts.

He commanded that the vaccine for small pox could not be given on the arm.

He objected them and then forced the doctors to give this vaccination in the gluteus maximus in the buttock rather than in the arm.

He then concluded, "You cannot have people mutilate patients in the name of science. You must be cautious, you must be sensitive of their looks and their aesthetics."

He also went further to say that in his view, non-clinical staff should never teach medical students.

Finally, he told us that microbiology is not different from cooking. You might be a great cook to be a great microbiologist.

***

When you see a hyena wearing the intestine of an animal as a belt, you must conclude that an elephant had died or had been killed. This was the feeling the students had when they went out for internships. For them, the moment they arrived at the outline station for their internship, they were received with great excitement and jubilation. This is despite the fact that during an internship, the intern or the new graduate is lowest in the pecking order of the medical autocracy. Salimo remembered that on one of those first days, when a guest arrived at the ward and inquired from the matron in charge, "Ma'am, is there a doctor on duty?" the answer from the matron was almost spontaneous, "No, there is no doctor, only an intern." To the establishment, an intern is not a doctor, he is a trainee who needs to be watched and only appreciated when nothing went wrong.

Indeed, as soon as Salimo arrived at this Lakeside city hospital, he was immediately put on a rotation in the maternity ward. Now, a maternity ward in the healthcare system can be regarded as the public relations front office for the institution. It tells the entire story of the life and goings-on in and out of the hospital. It is a place where hot medicine is practised. This is where the emergencies occur, which cannot wait. If the baby is in distress, you must postpone everything else in order to achieve the desired results of a live baby and a live and happy mother. Indeed, during this one year of intense scrutiny, activity and sleepless nights, if there is anything Salimo learned then it is the fact that, to save lives you must have sharp reflexes, you must make quick decisions and finally you must implement them appropriately.

Appropriately did not mean managing or treating the entire condition yourself. Sometimes or most of the time, since you're under supervision, it meant that you needed to make the right diagnosis using what in medicine is called diagnostic acumen, which in simple terms means take a good and thorough history, do an examination that is meticulous. Lastly, do or select the most appropriate investigation so that you can get the right diagnosis the first time.

In this kind of institution there was no luxury of technology, the most sophisticated piece of equipment was a light microscope, a plane X-Ray and later on during the year, the students were able to do dynamic studies like visualisation of the kidneys and the gastrointestinal tract using contrast. The next thing Salimo learned is that the best teachers for a young doctor were not necessarily the consultant or the specialist. Often it is the nurse, the midwife or the matron. Sometimes it could also be a theatre attendant.

Some of these theatre attendants have been in theatre for what Salimo's friend used to call donkey years. They know all the steps towards achieving successful results in an operation. At least the most common operations they could do if given a chance, only the law prohibited it. Salimo remembers that during this rotation, his aspiring partner was Sandhu, a nervous young man who knew everything in theory. When it came to doing it, he would go through three phases; a phase of denial, a phase of panic and finally a phase where everything fell together and he could go on with the procedure. There were several initiations to the process, which involved first you assisting the specialist, secondly you assisting the medical officer, thirdly the medical officer assisting you, and finally you doing the caesarean section yourself with the mid-wife or one of the other interns.

On this occasion, young Sandhu had said, "Today is my day," but nevertheless he implored Salimo. "Salimo, you must be next door, just in case I get into distress." His first point of distress was when he opened the abdomen of the heavily pregnant mother. Turning to his assistant, he asked, "Where is the uterus? Colleagues, where is the uterus?" He asked his colleagues again, much to the consternation of everybody in the theatre.

"The uterus is right in front of you," the nurse who was assisting indicated it, pointing and touching the fundus of the uterus. This is the moment when Sandhu Patel realised that he had actually gone through the necessary steps of exposing the uterus and the next step was to identify the bladder, safely get it out of the way and finally, meticulously make a transverse incision at the base of the uterus before gently massaging the baby, or pushing it out of the uterus.

From the moment Sandhu acknowledged that he had reached the uterus, everything fell into place but with the assistance of the theatre assistant who guided him through in a very responsible and precise manner, telling where he must cut, what he must avoid; most importantly, he must not damage the bladder, damage the uterus or even make his incisions so wide that he encroaches on the main arteries into the uterus, but finally his entry into the lumen of the uterus must be such that he doesn't cut the baby. Incidentally, it's not uncommon for the novice to, by being overzealous, not only cut the uterus thin myometrium and in the same stroke cut the covering of the baby, and in some not uncommon instances, even nick the forehead of the baby.

However, on this occasion, poor Sandhu was able to successfully conduct his first caesarean section. From there on he enjoyed every moment of his rotation in the Department of Obstetrics and Gynaecology. On Salimo's part, the first case that he encountered was a retained placenta. Indeed, again during their training they had been cautioned to say if there is a retained placenta, you must approach it with caution. It's one of the things that you will learn by heart. One, you don't yank it out of the uterus, you don't pull it and generally the fingers of the surgeon are the most important surgical instrument that you use under those circumstances.

Being Salimo's first case, he called his immediate supervisor, one Dr Alusiola and said, "Sir, we have a case of retained placenta. I need your assistance." The laughter from the other end of the line could be heard by everybody in theatre.

At the end when he was able to control himself he called Salimo and said, "Doc, if I were to come to the hospital every time there is a retained placenta, I will have no time to rest. In any event that is the bread and butter of a newly graduated doctor, that's yours... There are three or four things you must learn to do even with your closed eyes." He didn't went go to enumerate them as being, one; how to control bleeding after delivery, which he called postpartum haemorrhage, two; how to conduct or perform a caesarean section, three; how to resuscitate the baby and four; how to ensure that the mother is safe before the operation, during the operation and after the operation.

In short, he told Salimo, "When you're a doctor, you're also the companion, the anaesthetist, you're the friend, the patient and you're the companion to the parent, the relatives of the patient." He told Salimo "that's the hallmark of a good doctor, and the best instrument or skill you can have is one of communication." Indeed, he reminded him of yet another important saying, "The tongue can tell you everything including the diagnosis. Doc, always remember this," and with that he hung up.

Being a responsible intern, Salimo then turned to the midwife and explained how he might approach this vast event. She nodded and said, "I think if you approach it like that, you have nothing to fear." With that, Salimo was set on the successful road into an internship rotation in obstetrics and gynaecology and indeed, all his internship rotation.

It wasn't long before he realised that one; the scarce resource that the interns had in the hospital, which is very limited is theatre time, two; a lot of hot emergencies, essentially dramatic injuries happen around the end of the month and three; the fact that when you are on call as an intern, you covered all the departments of the hospital. The next important thing Salimo learned as an intern was that sleep was a luxury. A good intern was not expected to sleep for more than four or five hours a day. You slept next to your telephone; at that stage there was no mobile phone, there was only a telephone, which was fixed line and later on they introduced a police-like gadget that was used to summon you to the hospital in case there was emergency. In the end it boiled down to that as an intern you were better advised to spend your night in the hospital even you were not on call.

This approach ensured that by the time Salimo's period of internship ended he was a competent doctor, he felt confident to go out upon registration and practice for safe medicine for the rest of his life and have a fulfilling career in medicine. Not all interns had it easy. Indeed, for the second time he met his good friend doctor Olila, who was now his aspiring partner in another rotation. Upon receiving his first salary, indeed all the salaries were delayed for three months, which to the two was too long, Olila disappeared for about two weeks and when he reappeared he had no remorse and he was not ashamed to explain himself. "Why were you away for two weeks?"

His answer was quick and precise, "Sir, the amount of money we earned was so much that I had to go and safely deposit it with my parents and a little amount for myself in the bank before I could come back, and that process took me two weeks."

Indeed, the consultant had no reason to doubt how genuine this explanation was, however, in the interest of discipline and maintaining quality of work, the penalty for missing two weeks was to stay behind for two weeks during the end of the rotation. Their professional life as an intern was as exciting as their social life. Indeed, in this town they were like the second crop of interns, at that time they were just approaching their mid-20s, some were even below 24. Very soon you were a very popular young man in the city. You were able to pick and select your sweetheart for the entire period or part of the period. It wasn't uncommon soon to be entangled in love triangles.

Salimo does remember vividly one event where, in the greed for more and more he ventured into more than he could chew. He had just taken an afternoon off to be with his newly found 'chick' as they called them, and having had a successful encounter, as they called it, was now ready to go to the hospital in the late afternoon. He met his regular lady on the way into town but it was clear that from the way she looked at Salimo that she was pregnant with mischief. After a few pleasantries, she informed him that she was off to town and when she comes back, she will come to the house, clean and prepare for dinner. Salimo said, "Okay, I'll walk you back so that I can go and put the ingredients in the kitchen and confirm that everything is there for your cooking."

No sooner had Salimo arrived in the house and alerted his newfound chic that her life and enjoyment might be short-lived than Betty stormed into the bedroom. After a quick look at how unravelled the place was, she went for the neck of the new chic. Only Salimo's quick reflexes saved her from being strangled and her nimble limbs enabled her to escape imminent demise. This did not spare Salimo one hour of wrestling and breakages in the room. Indeed, after they had been wrestling inside, the hostilities extended onto the patio, in front of the house, which incidentally was overlooking the highway. This wrestling only ended when her good companion from the police department, who was taking a walk home, noticed some activity on the patio and diverted them. Walking in, what he noted was both comical and serious. After he restored peace he then asked what had happened, and upon explanation it was decided that it was in the interest of peace and harmony if Betty went to her home that day and then the next day they could resolve the matter.

Once the lady had left, the police officer could not restrain himself from long, prolonged laughter. Because upon examining Salimo, one his trousers was torn from navel to the ankle. He had many scratch marks and even bite marks. He then summoned Terry to come to Salimo's aid and administer all manner of preventive medicines including anti-tetanus toxoid. This police officer never stopped laughing, he said, "You know, I was passing and then I said, 'Oh, what function are they celebrating today, I see the doctor dancing on the patio'. On coming closer, I found it was something more serious than simply dancing, or a waltzing or a dance."

The next day, Betty arrived and being knowledgeable about drugs, she thought she must teach this doctor a lesson, and indeed this lesson was well learned, although not always effectively observed. She took a couple of Valium tablets and was asleep for easily 24 hours.

It wasn't the torture from the possibility that she could pass out as a result of this medication but as young doctors, both were fully aware that given the amount that she indicated she had swallowed, she would have a peaceful sleep, which in some case would be therapeutic. On the other hand, it meant Salimo would take care of her, deal with her toiletries, carry her to the toilet, and bring her back until she was ready to go home. Indeed that brought to end this unfortunate incident.

As for Joe, they used to tease him that it would appear that fever has no effect on fertility, contrary to what they read in books about the life of sperms. This is because they were documenting that on occasion his regular girl became pregnant following an encounter where Joe's temperature was hovering around 39 and 40°C. They were expecting him to throw up any time, but on the other hand what came to be was a pregnancy. They concluded that temperature has no effect on pregnancy, or at least outside the man's body, temperature does not deter pregnancy.

On another occasion, Joe was confronted with his young lady, the chic who was claiming that she was pregnant and had arrived at the hospital as an emergency coming from the city. Thereafter she was taken in for emergency treatment as a case of incomplete abortion. Little did they know, she had passed through some other clinic where they had taken blood from her vein and injected it into the reproductive canal before they set her on the way, as it were, to confound the interns, because as soon as she arrived and the intern recognised bleeding with clots, he diagnosed incomplete abortion. He proceeded to complete the abortion.

This did not convince their specialist, who on seeing that this lady was not from the neighbourhood, but probably from the city, noted that there was an unholy alliance and that this lady might have conned them all. He then went on to give her a very sharp tongue-lashing, which was extended also to Joe. Indeed at the end of it Joe was threatening to sue the specialist. As they knew, Joe was too much of a diplomat to engage in that kind of activity.

The only downside of their internship was the fact that they were not economically, sufficiently paid. Their salaries could not afford them a decent car or a holiday. However, the government in its wisdom, realised that if they hooked you as an intern and they hooked you as a medical officer you're likely to them the necessary services that support your education. The government organised a system where you could walk into any auto shop, pick a car of your choice and the government would underwrite the loan, which meant that you had to work for the government until every cent was paid. With this opportunity in mind, Salimo wasted no time in acquiring for himself his first car, an Alfa Romeo. A sexy car that complimented his age.

Salimo remembers that when the first instalment was taken, which had accumulated into three instalments by the time they were paying, his net pay for the month was two bob, which is two Kenya shillings. The cost of posting the pay slip was more than the amount of money that he earned for that month. He was not discouraged because now at least they could date with ease, they could drive with ease and would appear they led the life of a doctor. A doctor without a car was disaster. Salimo remembered that before this, they would go to town with his friend Henry, go to the market, and get one of the youngsters pushing a rickshaw. They would then go and purchase her wares including a banana and they would be walking behind this young man as he trekked the entire three kilometres to their flat to deliver the merchandise.

This is the life they had led for the first six to seven months. On arrival with this merchandise, Henry, who hailed from the neighbouring country where bananas were the prime meal, would prepare the most delicious boiled banana; better still, fried banana lunch, which he would spice the point that it was irresistible. Or occasionally with all that merchandise their specialist in child health, whom they knew also as a senior bachelor, would make *ugali*, which he had learned how to make better than any woman in Africa; or that's what they concluded. He would ensure it had the best consistency.

One of the phenomenon in Africa in cooking, is that there is no precision of ingredients. He knew how many people he was cooking for, therefore he put enough water from experience. When it has boiled, he'd put sufficient amount of maize flour; not too much as to make the whole process come to a premature end, but sufficient to make it continue to cook. He would then gradually increase the flour, and if the consistency was good enough for the entire pan to have resemblance of a cake inside. The senior cook, as they called him, would then cover the pot and let it simmer for a while. He would then take the pot by one hand; luckily it had a handle. He would turn it over and the entire cake would land on the tips of his five fingers, he would then drop it back into the pan, the top side now to be at the bottom.

When this *ugali* came out, after further baking, it was the most delicious *ugali* that one would ever enjoy. More so if it was eaten with the sauce that he would prepare in a special way and add just sufficient amount of pepper to make everything sizzling and delicious. Everything would be hot, 60 degrees centigrade and outside would be hot so you would be sweating both from the temperature in the atmosphere and the temperature of the food, but Salimo cannot imagine any time in his life that he enjoyed *ugali* more than a combination of what Ken, their specialist paediatrician could prepare together with the sauce he made himself.

Ken had one girlfriend. Not so much a girlfriend; no, Ken and Terry had dated the same young lady. After a nice meal, the young lady confessed that unknowingly she had come to the house of one and found two, she never knew that they shared a house, and didn't know how to deal with the situation. The sub-shooter, as they called him; Terry, struck first, transferring her to his room and coming back to finish the dinner. When Ken asked what was up, Terry explained to him that he had a date with this young damsel, as they called her – but better still, they knew her as Crankshaft or Bionics.

This was not in a derogatory manner but in awe. They held her in awe because despite having been affected by paralysis and having to walk on callipers, she had the most beautiful face that any young woman had at that age. She was also extremely sweet to talk to. Salimo remembers her for one thing; that disability is not inability, and that he was sure that despite her disabilities from polio, any of them could have married this young lady and continued to have a most exciting marital life thereafter. The next morning when they were being told about this double date, it was in a most inauspicious circumstance. Ken was narrating how in the middle of the night he had heard a commotion in Terry's room and let his imagination run wild, believing that it was

Crankshaft who was in danger. He was sure that someone had fallen out of bed, and was now waiting for a cry of pain and suffering. To his surprise there was neither a cry nor any evidence of pain.

This sharpened his curiosity the next morning, and he said, as normally they called each other: "Joe, I thought Crankshaft was in bad shape when I heard some commotion in your room; I was sure someone had fallen out of bed." With great laughter, Terry confessed that he was the one who had fallen out of bed in the course of the action.

Thereafter, Crankshaft, as they knew her, continued to frequent Terry's house with regular frequency and settled herself there as the lady of the house. This encounter of Crankshaft with Terry could have lasted forever except for one incident, where a police raid on some estate recovered, among other things, the identity card of Terry. Since this was a small city, it was revealed that a doctor's identity card was found on this estate and it was unclear under what circumstances this card had been misplaced.

No amount of explanation could console Crankshaft, for she had believed that Terry was as holy as an angel. At least, that's how he presented himself. Their one year of internship in this lakeside city ended sooner than they expected. Very soon the whole team of Joes would be reunited in Nairobi as post-graduate students. The entire internship period was full of action, full of drama and ended before any of them could fully absorb the major transformation that they had all undergone. They were indeed mature doctors. Salimo remembers that one of the seniors who had come to join them, Teddy, had done his internship in the major city hospital. During the first three or so months with them, they, the junior interns, were the ones assisting him to master the practical skills of a doctor.

This is why they felt very strongly of themselves when Joe declared that if you see a hyena using the intestine of an animal as a belt, then you must conclude that an elephant had been slaughtered. For them, as interns in that lakeside city, in terms of the clinical experience, it was indeed like an elephant had been killed. They had absolutely no competition for cases, they were given graduated responsibilities all the way to doing even regular routine operations. That's where their future specialisation was defined. For Salimo left knowing that he would be a surgeon.

Indeed, the amount of major operations and major trauma cases that he had managed was what most specialists would do over a lifetime.

This is not exaggeration. Salimo knew for a fact that during the year with the supporting the surgeon, he had performed no less than one hundred prostatectomy procedures. Many surgeons would do that over a period of four or five years if they are lucky. Being in a small, busy regional hospital, one had the advantage of being the "doctor". Salimo had acquired sufficient confidence to go through his post-graduate without too much worry; indeed, for all it is worth, what he knew he got from post-graduate were the principles of surgery, but the practice of surgery he had already completed during his internship. Indeed, he'd even gone further to excel in obstetrics.

At this stage, while they were trying to save on resources, time was of the essence, so they were competing on how long it took to complete a caesarean section. Going from skin to skin, as they called it, they had perfected the skill so much that it was hovering at 20 minutes, but by the time Salimo stopped doing the caesarean sections he was doing it at 15 minutes, meaning from the time you put knife to the skin to open the abdomen of the lady to the time you put the last stitch in putting the wound together, having safely delivered the baby, it was 15 minutes. This for them was a major achievement. They even prided themselves on reducing the amount of anaesthesia the baby is exposed to and reducing the morbidity associated with caesarean section to no more than 48 to 72 hours of bed rest. Indeed for them the mother would be already encouraged to walk or sit up in bed by 24 hours, the catheter would be removed towards the end of the 24 hours and she would be mobile in 48 hours. They would then discharge the mother to come back for removal of stitches, going home on the third day after the caesarean section.

On a cautionary note, this was for straightforward caesarean sections; either any obstructions had been anticipated and planned for and it was uncomplicated procedure and the mother was well prepared for the process. At the lakeside city, also they managed to discover the corners of the city; particularly the nightspots. There was, for example, Octopus, or as it was labelled at the entrance, Octopus Bottoms Up, a popular resort where you would find any manner of youth; male, female having the best time of their life. They, as interns from time to time when they were off, would frequent this spot during Saturday evening. Indeed, the ladies patronising there also had mapped out the city and since as a young doctor you didn't want to go home with a lady from this source, they made it easier for you to have the complete session in streets which the police never frequented.

Later on as a researcher, Salimo came back to Octopus Bottoms Up, this time not for entertainment but more for research. He was doing research that would lead to the development of a condom strategy for the country. That was much later as a trained specialist and as a researcher. Salimo could conclude that his virginity was lost at this Lakeside city both in the social definition and professional definition. He became a mature professional, having arrived there as essentially a mature adolescent in terms of the profession. In terms of his social development, that's where his life started. The takeaway message for them from that encounter was, the internship has to be handled with care; that's where you can lose yourself as a professional or you can make your career of the medical profession. That's where you get truly 'formatted' or 'configured' into a mature professional.

***

The only other notable thing which happened during their one-year internship was the death of the legendary Jomo Kenyatta. Salimo's memory of the day is vivid. He was engaged in performing a vacuum delivery at the maternity hospital. So engrossed was he in this event that the one o'clock news completely eluded him. It was only when he came out of the delivery room that he was informed by the anxious looks from the people in the hospital. And on inquiring, he learned that the reason why they were anxious was because news had filtered through, that the great one had passed away. They had become too used to his vibrant voice to expect his passing to happen as suddenly and unexpectedly as it did. Not that it was not expected, knowing his age and the fact that he was perpetually on holiday in Mombasa, which was described as a walking holiday at the coast.

On this particular day, and a few days before, he had been extremely busy up and down along the coast from Kilifi to Kwale, performing several kinds of ceremonies, marking the opening of important projects by the government. Therefore, when news came of his passing, everybody was totally dumbfounded, and everybody was worried about what would happen next. In their little town, people could be seen murmuring in corners and consulting. For them at the hospital, nothing much would have happened if it were not for their friend Tom, who was worried about his New Zealand girlfriend. Kate had introduced to them the use of capsicum, or green pepper. Until Kate came into the picture, they were never aware of the green pepper; they saw it, but it didn't interest them.

So when Kate, one day, appeared out of the blue and they were informed that she's their friend's girlfriend, they were extremely enthralled by this active and lively individual from New Zealand. To some of them, this was the first time they we were meeting someone from New Zealand. New Zealand, to them, was that island country so far away, that the chances of meeting anybody from that island were as remote as the passing of Jomo Kenyatta.

Tom was particularly worried because Kate was a foreigner and was in the country. She had travelled on her own to the coastal town where the legend had passed away. He was particularly worried because she had not called back, and there was no telephone contact through which he could connect with her. No amount of reassurance would convince him that Kate would be safe. His fear was founded on a common perception in the country that the passing of Jomo Kenyatta would cause a political tsunami in the country; there would be turmoil and tribal clashes. In short, there would be chaos in the country. Therefore, when this announcement came, the next thing they were expecting to hear was chaos, skirmishes and tribal animosity in the various parts of the country.

However, as the day wore on, and nothing seemed to happen, gradually, life in Kenya started taking on its natural rhythm. Not that Jomo Kenyatta controlled the rhythm. In fact, at some stage, Jomo Kenyatta had become more or less irrelevant. During the past few years, they only heard about Jomo Kenyatta during major public holidays; in June, during the Independence Day.

They also heard about Jomo Kenyatta in December, when they celebrated Jamhuri Day. In between, Jomo Kenyatta appeared during graduation ceremonies, as he was the chancellor to the only public university, the University of Nairobi. Other occasions when you heard about Jomo Kenyatta is when there was the shuffle of cabinet, or some important dignitary was arriving in the country. Usually at one o'clock, the only broadcaster – the government broadcaster, would suspend normal programs to bring what would have been termed as breaking news announcements. Then the national anthem would be played, followed by the voice, the booming voice of Jomo Kenyatta, usually starting with his favourite way of addressing Kenyans, 'ndugu zanguni', or 'My fellow countrymen' or, 'comrades'. He would then go on to briefly state what they had achieved until this time since he took over as the founding president. These would be followed by his brief announcement that was always punctuated with, "These changes take place with immediate effect".

To his credit, Jomo Kenyatta understood better than any of the presidents who followed after him, the importance of systems and consistence, experience and expertise, and most importantly, the value of education. The per capita highest qualifications attained by members of his cabinet were, surprisingly, extremely high. Many of his ministers were holders of university degrees, or even PhD degrees. There was one who was later known as ten percent. He was reputed to be one of the first Kenyans to have a PhD. There was the young minister for economic planning who had a PhD in economics. And many more. Indeed, it was a shock when Arap Moi took over from Jomo Kenyatta, and suddenly the average qualification of members of cabinet dropped by 50%. His argument was that nobody should be left out. That it was in the interest of equity to ensure that every corner of the country was represented at the level of minister, assistant minister or permanent secretary.

To Jomo Kenyatta, permanent really meant permanent. Indeed, there were some permanent secretaries who held these positions easily for 20-25 years, the entire lifetime of Jomo Kenyatta's administration, spilling over into Arap Moi's administration. At some stage, the firebrand politicians were complaining, "To Jomo Kenyatta, permanent really means permanent," because there were some permanent secretaries who had become too powerful, and it was claimed that they were untouchable. So Jomo Kenyatta never wavered in his belief that punishment for incompetence was moving them to another ministry, rather than firing them, but it became the order of the day in Arap Moi's government.

It's definitely not surprising that a lot of his ministers and permanent secretaries gained such a vast amount of experience. All of them, or a majority of them, continued to run the government long after Jomo Kenyatta was dead. Indeed, one of his youngest ministers eventually rose through the ministry of finance, economic minister of finance, to become yet another President for the Republic.

The death of Jomo Kenyatta did not change anything radically. The sun continued to rise from the east and set in the west. The rains continued to come at regular intervals. Indeed, much to the surprise of everybody else, the transitional period was very smooth. Immediately after the announcement, it was also announced that there had been a cabinet meeting which was chaired by the vice president, Arap Moi, and that during this meeting, he had been unanimously proposed as the new President of the Republic. This was a constitutional provision; it was no favour to Arap Moi, but it was equally surprising for Arap Moi because this had come from a very shaky background; very uncertain periods of time when there had been many attempts to create a transitional change in the constitution that would have seen Moi not take over as the President.

At one stage, there had been discussion in the parliament on the succession of Jomo Kenyatta. And it was clear to everybody who could read and write, hear and see, that the intention was to block the possibility or the likelihood that Moi could become the President of Kenya. Indeed, when he took over, there were those who would declare that this was a passing cloud. To their surprise, Moi outlasted Jomo Kenyatta as president. His presidency might be the record presidency in Kenya in terms of duration, easily two decades.

The circumstances of the passing of the legendary Jomo Kenyatta are unknown to everybody. The only thing which is known is that it was reported that he passed on peacefully during his sleep. However, as the time went by, the news started filtering that this was, after all, not as peaceful as it was said, nor was it during his sleep. Yes, he died in bed, but it was not as if this was a late night or gradual sequence of events in which the sage snoozed, gradually fell into deep sleep and never woke up the next morning. It was, however, accepted all round that Jomo Kenyatta died a natural death. In all natural deaths, the heart stops, and the rest of the organs of the body also stop.

In no time, Kate reappeared, safe and sound, unmolested and unruffled, happy and confident, as usual. Kate was even surprised that Tom was worried to death. "What do you think would happen to me, darling?" she asked Tom.

"Well, these are not easy times, these are difficult times, and we were expecting chaos as soon as it was announced that Jomo Kenyatta had passed on."

"Why would there be chaos?" Kate naively inquired.

"Well, you know the politics of tribalism, and the politics of succession" Tom tried to explain. One would expect that those tribes who complained of being marginalised, or who claimed that they should also have a taste of the presidency, would want to take over. But on the other hand, once in power, always in power. The ruling class from Jomo Kenyatta's tribe would not easily be expected to give away power. Therefore, it was always expected that there would be trouble. The expectation was not only internal, locally for Kenya, but this was widely the expectation internationally, and people were asking what would happen after Jomo Kenyatta, long even before his demise was announced.

To the credit of the Kenyans, there was no tsunami, there was no earthquake, everything continued in spite of the body of Jomo Kenyatta lying in state. He received one of the most highly ceremonious farewells in the presidential send off. Until many years later, it was the only presidential send off.

As stated earlier, the ascending to power of Toroitich Arap Moi was not expected. The infighting that culminated in a motion in parliament to discuss the succession of Jomo Kenyatta was the result of the insiders' understanding that Jomo Kenyatta would expire anytime. Or more accurately, those who knew that he had lost the capacity to govern many years back; that his health was not favouring his continued presidency. The discussion on succession went on unabated. At that moment when it was just about to boil over, none other than the equally legendary Charles Omae brought an abrupt end to discussion. In a press release, Charles cautioned Kenyans against plotting or imagining the death of the president. He informed Kenyans that it was a treasonable offense to talk of, imagine, or to think about the death of their president. The import was that discussion of the succession of Jomo Kenyatta in parliament was in some ways trying to think, or imagine the death of Jomo Kenyatta. With that announcement, and realising that the government of Jomo Kenyatta was not very friendly to these enemies, the discussion in parliament was terminated and never to be heard of, henceforth.

Charles is a man of many lives. His image during the life of Arap Moi even became bigger than life itself. He was the man behind the king. He had the ear of the President, and understood and propagated the message of the new president, which was described as the Nyayo philosophy. It was therefore surprising that it didn't take long for a commission of inquiry to be set to investigate the activities of Charles, particularly since he was being accused of trying to mastermind a coup in a far-off country, Seychelles, and also of plotting to overthrow the government of Arap Moi.

To his credit, Arap Moi did not act rashly; he did not order the arrest of Charles. Instead, he established a commission of inquiry into the activities of Charles. At the end of the commission's investigations, it was concluded that, yes, there was evidence that his activities were not totally honest. Arap Moi, true to his word, decided to grant amnesty to one of his closest allies and kingmaker, Charles. The commission of inquiry on Charles itself is a momentous event, and is engraved eternally in the history of Kenya.

With the death of Jomo Kenyatta, and the realisation that there would be life after Jomo Kenyatta, even the interns went back to their normal routine. They continued to enjoy the latitude of operation expertise that they were gaining at the expense of those who went into the bigger centre where they were competing with postgraduate students, with many more interns, and other junior doctors. For them, the moment their internship came to an end and they received the letter from Doctor Martin Luther Oduori, signed, 'Martin Luther Oduori', confirming that they were now registered as medical practitioners, they understood how much they had gained from this experience in the lakeside city.

This soon was to be followed by transfers into district hospitals and the other facilities. But for many of them, it also became clear that being registered as a general practitioner was not the end of life. They started to look around for the possibility of postgraduate training in Kenya and abroad. Salimo oscillated between paediatrics and child health, to obstetrics and gynaecology, but now settled in general surgery. He didn't want a long break between his internship and postgraduate specialisation.

One of the important things about their city was that it was a lakeside city, it was close to the only surviving equatorial forest in the country. But also, it had the dubious reputation that in one of its suburbs live, idle dogs were sold. Usually, people would go for puppies which they would want trained, or dogs which had been trained. But to go to an auction of dogs was unheard of. Indeed, during their stay as interns, they were compelled to travel to see what the sale of dogs entails. It was unimaginable to think that one could go to the market and buy with money that could otherwise only buy an elderly dog, one whose demeanour it did not know, and that the dog would be passive enough to be transferred from one owner to another without putting up a fight.

Indeed, when Salimo visited the market with his old friend Terry and others, and Joe, it was a normal market like you have for cattle. People were holding dogs by the chain, prospective buyers were examining the dogs one by one and they were deciding on the basis of colour, and whether it was healthy, more than whether it would serve the purposes of a guard dog. It was unclear what had been done to make these animals, which are normally fierce, so sedate. Or maybe their expectation of the dog was not consistent with the marketplace. They did not know that the market was not for wild dogs, dogs which would even be barking at the owners. This was a marketplace for friendly dogs, dogs that one could describe more like pets, or more precisely, as toy dogs, essentially, or scarecrow dogs.

None of them tried to find themselves a suitable dog. In any event, as an intern, you are unlikely to have the ability to take care of a dog, particularly attend to his needs, meals included.

Indeed, they had been warned when they arrived at this lakeside city, that it's unthinkable and unimaginable for an intern to try and raise a family, or a dream of getting married during the period. There was no likelihood that a marriage born out of an internship would last. Similarly, to conceive the idea of owning a dog and taking care of it successfully was also equally unimaginable. Nevertheless, they decided to go to see the dogs being auctioned at the favourite place, the only place where idle dogs were being auctioned in the whole of east and central Africa.

Did they try to go and see the equatorial forest? No, there was no time. To do it would take a boat ride or travel by the lakeshores to the other side. No, there was no time. In short, they were totally immersed interns, owned by the state, owned by the profession, owned by the patients and their families. For many of them who were adopted, that degree of acquiescence or self-denial was a most formative period of their time. Needless to say that out of the six or seven of them in the Joe group, only one of them went into private practice soon after specialisation. Osman, he's lost somewhere between the North Sea and England, continuing to dedicate his time and resources to the service of humanity. The last time they heard of him, he was said to be a successful surgical specialist in the area of trauma.

They also learned, unpredictably, that he was married to some kind of royalty in the United Kingdom. Unfortunately, his long silence had made it difficult to verify any of these claims, that he might have been knighted, or that he was still married to that royalty. All they knew and were sure of is that he successfully trained in the area of trauma, and he was a registrar and a specialist in trauma in many parts of the United Kingdom. He's one of those who responded effectively to the call in the song of male circumcision in Salimo's village: the young men are graduated to confront challenges in all four corners of the Earth: east, west, south, north, they are supposed to wage the war of progress in all these corners.

The coming into power of Arap Moi brought with it a wave of fresh air in the polluted political atmosphere. Jomo Kenyatta, who inherited a sophisticated political system with effective checks and balances, had spearheaded a devolved administrative structure with regional governments unable to comprehend its operational systems had gradually battered the system and dismantled it into a de facto dictatorship. The level of political intolerance was at all levels pervasive. Jomo Kenyatta was conforming to the prevailing *spirit* of "Made Easy", part of the title of newly released series of student texts in the country and the region. One read "Economics Made Easy"; another, "Business Management Studies Made Easy"; yet another read "Statistics Made Easy". For Jomo Kenyatta, this was "Government made easy!"

Indeed, when Arap Moi assumed power, one of his gestures for which he probably was to be most remembered for, as a mark of political maturity, was to release all political detainees and prisoners immediately. Once the amnesty was announced, out hobbled half-cripples, some of them on crutches, a result of a mixture of torture and physical neglect or impoverishment and malnutrition. If Jomo Kenyatta had been given leadership on a silver platter, Moi received it through a constitutional process. His understanding of government was one of control and suppression of pockets of dissent at any cost.

Jomo Kenyatta abolished popular debate, as this was always interpreted as challenging authority. To Jomo Kenyatta, the structure and working a chieftainship was the model of government. His regime was incapable of comprehending an opposition; how an opposition could be allowed to flourish later on de-funded from national budget. No wonder Jomo Kenyatta drew down the curtain of political maturity or civilisation, leading the country down a dangerous and slippery slope into an odious monolithic cliché.

Jomo Kenyatta had promulgated into law a unitary state with one political party and a chessboard of the imperial system and the Chinese Communist Party approach all mashed into one. To be fair to Jomo Kenyatta, even the Americans are unable to comprehend the working of a multiparty system, and still retain a semblance of imperialism under the Electoral College system as a mechanism of preserving the aristocracy. Regardless, the passing of Jomo Kenyatta expanded the political space infinitely, albeit for a brief moment before Moi rolled the carpet right back to the wisdom of Jomo Kenyatta. After all, he declared that he would pursue the Nyayo philosophy, meaning he would follow the footsteps of Jomo Kenyatta. The icing on the cake of Jomo

Kenyatta's regime, was the pomp and ceremony surrounding his funeral and eventual burial in a mausoleum. This followed a procession across the streets of Nairobi of the horse-drawn casket to Uhuru Park where the church ceremony would be conducted. The event smelled of imperial coronation rather than a burial or a final send off, a final hero's send off. Jomo Kenyatta's government was largely exclusionist. It was never intended to be inclusive. One only needs to read what came to be the party manifesto, as spelled out in the sessional paper number 10 on African Socialism and its application to economic development, authored by one Tom Mboya, to realise that.

This document gives a clear understanding of the narrow interests provided for by the government of Jomo Kenyatta. Indeed, the central theme was they would invest in urgent resources in the high potential areas of the country. The core of that meant that the low potential areas, particularly the barren North, would not be of interest to the government. Only Barrack Senior dared to rubbish the document. Needless to say, when he passed on, there was no whimper in the country. The newspapers on their part covered the event in the inside pages while on the breaking news were much more mundane matters like the passing away of a young artist following a falling rock.

***

The end of the internship marked for them the start of a new era. Immediately, the Joe Group reconvened in the city to start a new four-year period of togetherness as they each wanted to specialise in different fields of medicine.

For Salimo, going against the advice from his mentor Professor Muanji; he abandoned any efforts to study psychiatry and went for the knife.

As the saying goes, "*Mguu wa Nyangau ndiyo jembe lake*".

Meaning, in good English, "The hyena's leg is the implement for cultivating."

For Salimo, his hands were soon to be transformed into the tool and implement for his livelihood.

He studied surgery previously during the one-year stint of his internship. He tooled his hands to be his spade, to be his shovel, to be his means of cultivating in medicine.

All he needed, therefore, were additional skills to tell him where and when cultivating should happen, where the hard rock is, where the soft soil is, where it is dangerous, and where it is beneficial both to the patient and the public, to intervene.

Joe decided to pursue his cause of paediatrics.

Notwithstanding their encounter and teasing, his long-forgotten sweetheart.

Sagini, like Salimo, resolved to go for the knife. Jim decided to also pursue the course in paediatrics.

Teddy, for the love of women, decided to specialise in obstetrics and gynaecology. Otis decided to go for public health.

So all in all, the Joe Group could effectively manage a hospital in all these specialties.

The tipping moment for Salimo to go in the surgical discipline was his observation that obstetrics and gynaecology was highly risky; not in the actual practice, but there was too much temptation of getting rich quickly.

At that time, abortion was, as it is today, illegal in Kenya. There were a lot of back-street abortions in the country.

Many young doctors specialising in the subject of obstetrics and gynaecology were falling prey to the temptation and many of them were finding themselves on the wrong side of the law.

Having observed these trends and not too sure how to be fully protected, through professionalism and served discipline, Salimo decided that it was safer to do general surgery. Indeed, Joe reinforced Salimo's resolve when he asked, "After you have learned how to successfully carry out a hysterectomy, what other challenge is there in obstetrics and gynaecology?"

To him, the softer disciplines, as they called them; medicine, paediatrics, and probably psychiatry, were where there was a challenge. Here there were unlimited fields of development, growth, learning and super-specialisation, as he explained.

To him, medicine is unchartered territory and one is better off when one goes to a field where there are not too many decoys; where the procedures are not fixed, where one is not constrained to think out of the box, to act out of the box, as he explained. To him, obstetrics was the smallest of the specialties, at least during that time. He would explain, "You know, at one moment in time, obstetrics was a specialty of general surgery.

"It's only in recent times that it has been necessary to recognise this profession which was initially a field for midwives."

As for him, although he had been declared to have the fingers of a surgeon, he found surgery not that exciting.

It suffered from the same limitations of open exploration, to think out of the box. "Joe," he was asking Salimo, "There are only a limited numbers of ways of opening up the abdomen."

"Now that you have learned all this technique of going into the abdomen, you have learned how to remove organs in the abdomen, how to know which organs they are, what more is there left for you to do?" He would ask.

In some ways, Joe was prophetic regarding endoscopic surgery, a nest that is gradually encroaching on the territory of surgeons.

The radiologists are equally encroaching on the space of surgeons, with respect to the brain.

But still, robotics are doing a better job in some procedures, particularly in the field of surgery.

Therefore, considerably, those aspects of surgery which define the men from the boys; dexterity, as they were referred to, are gradually becoming obsolete.

However, having gone into that profession, suddenly Salimo realised that there was a huge space around the surgeon.

Therefore, Salimo never regretted this choice.

From time to time, the Joe Group met to exchange notes.

The Joe Group often shared weekends, public holidays, and events such as going to soccer.

The Joe Group once more found themselves thinking big, thinking of transformation, thinking of changing health care delivered in the country.

Jima wondered one day, "Simon, do you remember how I one day declared that we guys appeared to be destined to manage the profession rather than to walk in the profession?" Indeed, for them, it was not a question of managing the profession, or managing administering the services. No. It was a question of transforming and modernising health care delivery and organisation in the country.

They were the kind of people who wanted to start from the profession itself, the professional association, to the management of the facilities, to their legislative bodies. Indeed, soon, they found themselves deeply embroiled in the politics of their medical association, in the politics of the enumeration and the conditions and times of work for head professionals, more so doctors.

Soon, they were in direct confrontation with the powers that be, particularly the government of the Toroitich Arap Moi.

Therefore, their communal converging in the city during their post-graduate brought them even closer together than when they were in medical school. This was despite the fact that they were engaged in specialisation in diverse fields of medicine.

More than dividing them, this diversification in the specialisation, brought them together to share different experiences and to complement each other, particularly when a patient need to be referred across disciplines.

Their first endeavour as they started to grow was to transform the medical association, so they all registered in it. They had registered in the association as medical students, but now they wanted to be at the forefront of its management.

Here, they realised that they didn't constitute a critical mass to make fundamental change at once or to revolutionise how the provision was administered.

They therefore decided to do it in two stages.

Initially, they would sponsor candidates who would be electable to lead the association.

They had noted that since independence, the leadership of the medical association remained in the hands of a small clique of older guards, as they called them.

Here was a prestigious association that for now several years had successfully published a renowned scientific journal, earning itself a lot of respect in the country.

So the first thing they did, during the first year they were in the city, having already converged, was to identify whom they should sponsor as the chair, whom should they sponsor as the secretary and how they would achieve this revolution quietly.

They realised that the leadership normally was not open to nominations, so they would send out one denomination for people to hold legislative positions, but the information would be circulated within the small group that was monopolising the organisation.

They therefore decided that in the next election, which was going to be held at the coastal city of Mombasa, the younger doctors would be there in big numbers, and they would insist on discrediting the nomination that had been clandestinely invited.

They would therefore change and say that they wanted to nominate from the floor.

After a brief debate, it was clear that among the audience there were sufficient numbers to nullify the secret ballot which had been proposed, to disqualify the nominations which had been received, and to nominate from the floor.

For the chair, they had identified their good old friend Yusufu.

And for the secretary, they had also identified a young physician who promised to deliver.

When their old professor confronted them about why they were not nominating him, they were equally honest with him. They said, "Sir, what excuse should we give the electorate to be willing to vote for you?

"It appears that merely telling them that you are our professor will not get you elected. They want the leadership that has track record in leadership that can deliver. So far, there is no evidence that you could do either of the two."

He was shocked and surprised, but he agreed with them that the time for change was now and change started on that day.

***

For the Joe group as they came to be known, converging in the city of Nairobi was more of a continuation of where they left at the time of undergraduate. Very quickly they teamed up as a group, and started pursuing the postgraduate training with zeal. But before continuing, they had to look into the supporting pillars of this training. In particular, they had to find suitable accommodation, find suitable girlfriends, preferably ones who would become their future spouses, and lastly establish a new routine of their activities in and out of the training environment.

In relation to the accommodation, they were more than ambitious. Notwithstanding that none of them was married; they nevertheless wanted to have housing that befits a registrar or a trainee specialist. At this time, there was not sufficient accommodation within the hospital environment, and they were left to their own devices. As usual, they did not accept this traditional approach to solving common problems that required each of them fend for himself. They decided that they might come to change some of the old traditions that continued to hamper progress.

One of these was that, the teaching hospital did not take sufficient steps to expand residential facilities, either for internship or for postgraduate training in line with the increasing number of trainees. They therefore decided that, the best course of action was to engage with the management to create additional space, or to expand space. To achieve this, they formed a Lose Hospital Doctors Association for the teaching hospital, to which Masaii was elected the secretary. They needed an acceptable a chair who couldn't appear radical, so radical as to scare the old guards as they called them. So indeed they got one Akuabi to be the chair. And what a chair they had found.

At their first meeting, they resolved that this group would become their de facto association for championing their own course, as well as those of the patients under their care. Their first agenda was to approach the hospital administration and demand a suitable accommodation within easy reach of the facility as most of them didn't have personal cars, but they were expected to be on call, and therefore they needed to be within easy reach even within walking distance. After several long and irritating sessions, the management challenged them to identify suitable accommodation within the neighbourhood that they would rent.

Very quickly they identified such accommodation and they were all of them settled not in the same estate but in different estates of the city, that were within reach of the facility. Needless to say, each ended up with a three or four-bedroom flat that was obviously an extravagant use of space, and looking back the whole Joe group should probably have just taken one flat. However, at that stage they were rather ambitious and had inflated egos, demanding that at their age they not share accommodation across the board.

Housing having been settled at the cost of the employer, they now gave themselves time to address issues of their future spouses. Joe found himself a new girlfriend and Pitt found himself a new girlfriend who came to be known as Warm Shoes.

Secondly, they now established a usual routine that on Friday they would meet in one of the Joes' houses, and map out what would happen during the weekend if they were not on call. Naturally, this would end up being a soccer match on Saturday or Sunday, and from time to time Otis would nose out for a party so that they were not confined only to seeing patients.

The next item which took centre stage was taking over the Medical Association. For a long time they had recognised that it was managed in an old-fashioned manner: it did not serve the interest of the younger doctors, and had no agenda for the future. One of these days, they were discussing the fate of their association when Jim noted that, according to the Newton's three laws of motion, the association needed to be awakened. Otherwise, as the first law stated, anybody would remain in a state of perpetual inertia or immobility, unless acted upon by external forces.

"Joe, do you know that according to Newton's first law of motion, every object persists in its state of rest or uniform motion in a straight line unless it is compelled to change that state by forces exerted upon it. And so it is with our association. At the moment it is in a complete state of rest, it's not even in motion," he concluded, "this situation requires changing this state by external forces."

"And who are these external forces?" Masaii asked.

The answer was almost unanimous. "We are the external force to change the course of the medical profession in this country. It's our responsibility." Joe added, "To ensure that we transform the health profession. We must transform it."

And now, armed with this notion that those laws of physics can be applied in a social context, they constituted themselves into an advocacy group amongst young doctors, the challenge; to disturb the old order that continued to disengage with reality on the ground. The reality on the ground was that one; younger doctors got a raw deal. Two, that the conditions of the public facilities left a lot to be desired, to use the word of the politicians. In all these things the profession association remained silent, but more importantly it appeared to collude with the politicians whose agenda they had distilled down to sell interests.

They also saw that for health in the country to be universal and for everybody to access health, there needed to be a new direction and this new direction was not going to come from the government itself. In reality, the prevailing social norm among health professionals was that if you can't change it, you ship out. And so often once you graduated and you were registered as a doctor, you set up a kiosk or a one-man shop in the corner of town because you could not compete with the old guards who were in the centre of town. And they found this unacceptable that in their own free country the people who benefited in the colonial era continued to occupy the prime places of private practice in the city, and the younger doctors were relegated to the outskirts or to the rural districts. Or so they thought.

They decided that their platform for making this change of bringing social justice, as they thought of it at that time in the country, in the health sector, in health in general, was their professional association. After many, long sessions of discussions and conjectures and dreams, they decided that you cannot challenge an established order, one; if you're poor, two; you're an individual, three; you have no vision.

Therefore, they had to have a platform, which was the association and the association had to have a vision and an agenda.

As happened from time to time after the first week in their specialisation endeavours, they converged in one of their flats and there being good music and good food, they'd indulge in what they considered loafer's lifestyle. Loafers or those without care – indeed they were more like, "Well things are bad out there but Hakuna Matata." That they didn't have to break their hearts and necks to change but they needed to have a way forward. They concluded that the first thing to do was to take over the leadership of the association. The second thing was to have an agenda for the new reformed association. And the agenda would revolve around the following things: one; that they needed social protection for the younger professionals and younger doctors, two; they needed to engage and to put pressure on the politicians.

They also concluded that you cannot make an impact if you're poor. And by definition, the medical association was impoverished, it had no resources. Jim contended that if you're poor, nobody will listen to you. "You have no voice, a poor man has no voice," he would say. Obviously he had made a lot of observations. At that time he also brought them the information to illustrate his point; he told them a story of this tough-talking, politically agitated village elder that rose to become the local chief and those days local chief was a very powerful person who collected tax using every means, including force.

It is said that the name of the person was Ochuodho. Ochuodho in the local language also meant essentially waste or dirt. Ochuodho was speaking very tough in one of the meetings and criticising the local administration when the local politician tapped him on the shoulder and said, "Hey, you better watch what you're saying. Do you know how you got to this post?" Ochuodho was paralysed for an answer because this was in a public forum. The politician who was sitting on his chair then took his pipe and, striking it around the heel of his shoe, informed Ochuodho that when the decision was taken for Ochuodho to be appointed as a local chief, he the politician was smoking his pipe and hitting it on his heel in higher places, therefore Ochuodho had better watch out.

Jim therefore concluded that young doctors can make as much noise as they want, but if they have no buying power, nobody will listen to them. It was on one of these occasions that they conceptualised three strategies out of this quagmire, as Jim described it; namely, they created a local medical protection scheme. They argued that in this way, they we could create an economic base for the association. Moreover they'll reduce the premiums and make them competitive compared to where their colleagues were taking this premium in Europe. Salimo was given the responsibility to study this and advanced a course for a local medical protection scheme.

They also realised that one of the bottlenecks to advancement, particularly when you're an African is if you don't have land, you don't have a house of your own and your children cannot go to school. Jimmy used to argue that give an African a piece of land – it doesn't matter whether it's in a swamp – enable him or her to have a house or a roof over his head, as he put it, and create good schools for his children, he will serve you faithfully henceforth and ever more. They in consultation selected one, Yusuf, a senior doctor who identified himself with the young doctors. They dreamt of a time when they would have their own society or cooperative society of doctors pulling together the meagre resources, as they put it, and eventually being credible enough to go to a bank or a financial institution and take a loan to build houses that young doctors could afford.

Jimmy was given the responsibility to create a cooperative movement. Thirdly, they needed to wrestle power out of the old guards. Big Joe, as they called him, was given the responsibility to come up with a plan on how to take power from the old guard. One other aspect which they thought was important to succeed was that they needed their own newsletter. Joe had figured out that every successful institution or organisation can be brought to its knees by the people who control the media; the people who communicate to the masses, and therefore they wanted their message to be heard. They wanted to transform the association; they needed to have their own newsletter.

Already the association had a journal, the East African Medical Journal but that journal was not accessible in content to the public or even to the junior doctors. And so they agreed that it will be necessary to have their newsletter. They also gave each other deadlines to show evidence that they were productive. Their launching pad was the forthcoming election of officials and having started the change, they were now able to elect their good old friend Yusuf to be the chair of this organisation essentially for unlimited time. They then put the first item on the agenda, one was that they would like to have their own newsletter.

The motion was carried without any opposition. They also moved that they need to study ways of creating a local medical insurance scheme. Once more it was not difficult to convince the people, or the masses as they called them, because the premiums which were being paid particularly to the United Kingdom were prohibitive and that tended to create a class society among doctors. Salimo then got the mandate to go ahead and do something. They also proposed in this very meeting that they need to have a cooperative society of the association. And Jimmy was given the responsibility to look at the legal pathways to having this society.

No sooner than Salimo occupied his position, he came out with a written proposal on the medical scheme and since it was modelled on the UK scheme, the association did not have to register a different company since they were already registered as a company. And so with a few of his friends, including his old university comrade, Sir Ben as they called him, they immediately produced the policy document and Salimo and his brother spent Christmas period mailing these forms to all practitioners in the country. To the great surprise of everybody, by March the registration had reached 1,000. There were only 1,500 in the country, and they had managed to attract 1,000 of them and indeed now within the association's assets, they could boast of having one million Kenya shillings in the account.

This was a major asset considering that at that stage, there was virtually no difference between the Kenyan Pound and the Sterling Pound. This was a major coup, so to say, in terms of creating their own capital base. Unfortunately, they learned through a painful history of this self-capitalisation endeavour. As soon as commercial insurance heard of their breakthrough, they became very marketable, and they were like brides and there were several established firms wishing to engage with them to run this business in a much more professional way and to make it sustainable. They learned lesson number one; being idealistic doesn't help, you must be both idealistic and pragmatic.

If they had taken one of these potential suitors, and partnered, that medical protection scheme would have been highly successful, or it would have not taken as long as it took to re-launch it. One suitor gave them a proposition of self-independence in 10 years, with good charts and graphs on PowerPoint, which was becoming fashionable. They were very impressed, but Jimmy, who was more revolutionary and more nationalistic, disqualified these engagements with the essentially foreign-owned companies as not consistent with the Joes' ideals of total emancipation of the country. Therefore, they lost the opportunity of getting a strategic partner to hitchhike their idea.

This endeavour of medical insurance only lasted two years, and the third year, the same commercial companies and the same companies from Europe convinced hospitals in the city not to recognise this locally managed scheme as being sustainable. Indeed there was a chorus from the old doctors who said, "Only one case of litigation and the whole capital base would wiped out, even the Kenyan Medical Association would need to be auctioned."

Indeed they convinced those who controlled the finances in the country and the policy to transfer all the premiums to the medical protection schemes in the UK so that they were cushioned. This was a painful lesson for them, but they learned something. Indeed, when the association re-launched this particular scheme a decade later, it became highly successful to the extent that it now expanded to include motorcar insurance, life insurance, every form of insurance, particularly one which was focused or directed towards getting the younger doctors to become successful in the profession.

As with the issue of the mouthpiece for the association, Joe was also a very good writer, in fact in his earlier days he had been a reporter for one successful daily in town. Indeed he used to boast, "Do you know that I interviewed Bush the senior when he was still in the CIA?" They did not know what this meant, but sure enough he produced a headlined article written by Joe himself. Gradually, Joe and Salimo partnered, but Salimo was perceived as the operative, the person who drives the agenda which has been set. He had a way of persisting and finding keys to closed doors. Joe propagated the idea of the newsletter, conceptualised it and Salimo was given the responsibility to work with him to produce the first issue.

Obviously the association at this stage was very poor, all they did was give them support and give them a letter of introduction. Joe and Salimo then embarked on fundraising for the association through advertisements. Salimo and Joe then identified writers, challenged them to write convincing articles, relevant to the profession and in support of their agenda. They even identified one of the ophthalmologist in the making, Masinde, to produce a hilarious column which was much cherished. They also got a cartoonist to support the process. Within two to three months, the two had managed to commit sufficient companies to put adverts in this newsletter which was focused on doctors, enough for them to hire a manager.

For an office, the group decided to use the hospices of the scientific channel that had been established almost 50 years prior. Medicus was conceived and delivered by the Joe group. Medicus became a formidable newsletter over the years. Once more, it did not contain the natural ingredients for perpetual success, but while it lasted, it always looked for medical news. At this highest point, Medicus was quoted internationally when the newsletter put up a story of a mega scandal involving tendering and issuance of tenders for pharmaceuticals. Indeed this story would lead Salimo into the doorsteps of the state house a few years later. The newsletter had even a scientific column. They had an editorial board. It was no coincidence that that group which they called themselves ENOS found themselves once more as members of the editorial board.

Jimmy, very soon, through the Ministry of Cooperative Development, managed to develop a constitution that was convincing enough to be registered with the ministry. Soon doctors were being encouraged to enrol in this social society, the Housing Cooperative Society as they called it. The first hurdle for this society was to find suitable land in the city and different towns, and to engage at low cost a team of architects who would develop plans for their society at cheap rates and do it in a manner that the houses that were produced did not cost more than, at that time, half a million Kenya Shillings or £25,000.

The way it was conceptualised, it was to sketch a four-bedroom house whose value would be probably £50,000, but develop it in stages; one bedroom, sitting room and kitchen or two bedrooms, sitting room and kitchen, to be delivered at the end of two years and the individual would already incorporate into the plan, two more bedrooms that they could add at their own cost. Through this arrangement which Yusuf popularised, soon it was possible to get the Co-operative Bank to advance the capital to develop the first 100 units.

This was a milestone in the history of the nation. A poor doctors' association, young doctors with no capital, whose salary at that stage was no more than KES1,500, which was about £75 at that stage, were starting to own houses. Indeed this became a model to be pursued by other professions, by universities and other entities through the mechanism of a members' cooperative society that goes on a check-off system, that creates enough financial capital to qualify for major loan or to use its own capital to loan to members.

This concept is glaring even 20, 30 years after the original thoughts were put on paper. The next thing is that the Joe group and now the new leadership under Yusuf, recognised that the association did not have a home; they had no office. Conchad came up with the idea of paying a visit to the patrons in the city; the city fathers. Obviously the biggest of the city fathers was Arap Moi himself. Yusuf had a way of getting around to power.

Indeed in his earlier days, being of Asian extraction, he had privileged status in the country and did not use it unwisely, indeed he used it very wisely to work with the freedom fighters, one of them already talked of before. In this case, they encouraged him to engage with Arap Moi and to convince him to provide one of the government houses in the city which had become a way of buying favours for the government, and since they were a non-profit making organisation, a social group, they probably qualified to get such a property at low cost.

The first time Yusuf talked to Arap Moi, his minders informed him that no ... Actually, the association had been given land previously, prime land overlooking Uhuru Highway and the City and therefore were no longer deserving because they had the land. They were shocked to learn that there was such a thing as land for the association which had been issued several years before. A quick check with the registrar of societies found that a counterfeit organisation had been registered and former officials of the association together with politicians had fraudulently transferred this land into their new company. That time the Joes group also learned the second lesson. Things are not what they appear to be at first sight.

Indeed, Jimmy extended this to their social life. He says, "The most beautiful woman is not obviously seen the first time. You need more than one encounter with the woman, to actually recognise the deep-seated beauty," that's how he put it. "Beauty is not seen by a glance." They learned that there's an underworld, and this underworld is not visible. When they assessed the power brokers who had taken the land from the association, Joe was very much the one leading the arguments, that it would be futile to lay claim to this land given that they were still very powerful individuals in society.

It was therefore prudent to go back to Arap Moi and explain that they had lost this land out of negligence or because they did not develop it and whether they would kindly consider and give a second one. Arap Moi, to his credit, he had many failings as it will become clear with time, but when a good case was presented to him, he was a good listener and he was action-oriented. Indeed, soon Yusuf emerged with an allotment letter entitling the association to prime land next to a famous club in Nairobi. Armed with this land, and with a cooperative society, having their own newsletter, at that stage also running a successful medical protection scheme in the country, the association was by far a most cherished institution in the country, unlike any other professional association in the country.

Only the East African Professional Society could boast of having the same clout at that stage. At the end of the year when the Joe group took stock as the elections were coming, it was clear that the revolution which had been conceptualised in Joe's room had succeeded beyond expectation. They were now challenged to contribute to this association, to contribute to the medical society and to manage and run this newsletter.

The newsletter was more or less a self-help scheme, but it was always successful in getting adverts that financed its operations and enabled them, or the association to hire people to run the newsletter. Those were the days before the desktop; it was the days before all these fancy programs for typesetting. Typesetting was done manually, and the processes were very defined; they would get people to write the article, type them on a manual typewriter, go to an agency where the plates are produced and typeset there, get them to do the plates and go to another printer where offset printing was possible.

In that way, Joe and Salimo would do most of the processes that are associated with typesetting, all the way to the camera-ready material as Joe would put it, and then take this for offset printing at low cost. The journal lasted 10 years, and in those 10 years, it had wide readership, it had a wide subscription and it attracted a lot of resources to the association.

Their cooperative society was self-maintaining; indeed it conformed to Newton's second law of motion, that the rate of change of momentum of a body is directly proportional to the force applied, and this change in momentum takes place in the direction of the applied force. For them, they explained that the cooperative society had acquired a momentum; they, having set it in motion, and that there was enough volume of business which constituted the force, and that they were always moving towards success.

More units were being developed, more of the regions or the branches of the association were buying into the idea, and generally they were headed in the direction of their revolution. Indeed they were now able to say they were moving at a high speed, their velocity as they saw it at that stage was what they wanted to maintain; they did not want to fall back, they wanted these houses. Every new doctor who comes out of Medical School has the capacity, immediately to own what he calls his own house, his own home. They were always looking back and assessing where they might be falling back or losing momentum. When was their mass of doctors, the group, becoming smaller, and what was the purchasing power? They did not want to revert to the zero option where they would remain stagnant, or they'd only develop in one city. They wanted the movement to be felt countrywide; ultimately they wanted to challenge the powers to bring a new social order in health.

Indeed a recurring discussion amongst them was the exploitation of poor Kenyans by the politicians and the private sector doctors. Little did they realise that without the private sector, the entire health sector would collapse. The healthcare would collapse if the private sector folded up. Then they learned yet another lesson that a nation develops to the extent that all its sectors are balanced, that the private sector has a role to play, and the public sector has a role to play, and that the two of them are mutually interrelated; they are not mutually exclusive, they eternally intertwine.

Unfortunately, as Garaj's friend later would say, "Yes, the concept of public-private partnership is highly developed in Kenya, but" he would add, "it's only developed in the pervasive way," that corruption in his view was a highly developed public-private partnership enterprise in the country. He lamented, "If only black people would convert the propulsive power of public-private partnership in a positive engagement, the nation would be highly developed."

***

During this first year, although ordinarily one would expect that the Joe group had gone beyond the age of love triangles that you would encounter with teenagers, from time to time, it did happen. During the first year, Sagini – who had families, what a new find, initially would call "The Indian Lady" – found himself embroiled in a serious confrontation between himself and the two ladies. The Indian lady was so named because she had been invited to a dance floor by Pete, and the song was "Bye-Bye, Indian Lady". It was among the top 10 at that time.

As they called it, Joe was having a good time. Sagini was having a good time, and when he was spied on, Joe noted that he was like one in a trance, and was playing the melodies on an imaginary guitar, and the back of this lady, and Joe could not help but fix his eyes on them for a little longer to understand, comprehend the emotion that was being transmitted between the two.

After the end of the song, during the break, Joe went to him and said, "Hey, Sagini. That was great, you were really cuddling."

"Ah, you know, the music was going all the way into the bone marrow," he explained.

"Yeah, it is the Indian lady, you know." She got the name "Indian Lady" during one of the following months. The whole Joe group had gone to the residential hall for the women at the university, commonly known as "The Box". The time out from "The Box" was 10:00. So when three of the Joe group arrived there, they went to Sagini's regular lady. After a few presenters, the lady brought in some coffee and some refreshments, Sagini excused himself. He was gone for easily one hour, probably one and a half hours before it was noticed that he had stayed wherever he went. And soon, it was approaching the time when cockroaches would be smoked out, as was the saying of the residents. This was 10 PM, when visitors are no longer entertained in these rooms.

For lack of a good explanation, it was decided that Sagini was lost, or he had found involvement in some emergency, and probably had to go back to the med school. So, together with the chauffeur, a friend of Sagini, who had accompanied them to once see Sagini's girlfriend, they drove back to the med school, and at the med school, they checked in his room. He was not there. In the meantime, his madam was getting frantic, she was fretting about what might have happened to him.

"Is he in some sort of trouble?"

None of them could explain this odd behaviour from their friend. So much to their embarrassment, it was agreed that they should go back and retrace the steps of Sagini from the hostel; maybe they would sniff his footprints. They then, fortunately, drove back, again the same way, to the hostel and at their destination. They could see a mass of lovers walking along what would now be called the Lover's Lane. Sagini had his hand around the waist of the Indian lady, walking like he had reached the end of his dream.

There was utter silence, complete silence, in the car. As soon as Sagini's regular lady comprehended what had happened, she did not even wait for the car to stop. She rushed out and went for Sagini as a caller. She was ranting and wailing and making all kinds of cries, among them "What is wrong with you? What are you doing to me? Why did you have to do it here?" On and on she went, and Sagini had no answer for any of those questions.

These would no doubt have gone on even longer, had the Indian lady not intervened, and informed Sagini she was not prepared to endure any more of this. In any event, she was feeling cold, and she wanted to go in and get warm shoes. They were all flabbergasted at this, considering the drama around them and her, that she was still cool and unperturbed, just observing these events as if they didn't concern her. And for her to complain of feeling cold that she wanted to go in and put on warm shoes, at the heart of this turmoil, was incomprehensible. And hence, her new name was generated, which transformed her from 'Indian Lady' to 'Warm Shoes'.

Obviously, it was not an occasion they cherished, they needed to bring it in to prevent a big audience coming to witness what had happened. Indeed, being at the front of the hostel, they had attracted a lot of attention. The noise of the truck and the commotion attracted a lot of attention and they thought it would be improper to continue staying there. So they were able to convince Joe Sagini's regular lady that what was required at this stage was a cool mind, and to bring Sagini to some kind of justice, to put him to task. How could he do this, knowing he was the one who brought all of them to see this particular lady!

They then agreed that the best thing was to assume that Sagini was lost or otherwise confused in some way, and for all of them to go back to Sagini's room at the med school. Having gone back after some struggle, it was possible to ask the regular lady to get into the room and wait for Sagini to arrive for her to get straight answers as to what he was up to. Kind of pacified, she settled in the room and the rest of group went away, shocked at what had happened in that short span of time.

It's clear that it was not difficult to explain why Joe would want to go to see his girlfriend and abandon them there and go to see his new find. Nevertheless, after the next day they went to check on the lady and found that Sagini had not come back and she was peacefully in bed. Later in the day, Sagini arrived. In his characteristic manner, he walked in with an aura of normalcy as if nothing had happened. His attitude always was, "it could have been worse! So why worry!" In his view, nothing matters to a man who says, nothing matters. More like for him, *hakuna matata*. Soon this became the mantra for the group: "Hakuna matata", the panacea for all ills. That life was tough enough, that to worry about everything that happens, you worry to death.

Well, as the saying goes, any two people whose navels have touched should be left alone. Or, more accurately, nobody should intervene in matters involving two people whose navels have touched. To this day, nobody has ever explained to us how Sagini and the lady were able to restore peace and move on like nothing ever happened. Needless to say, neither of these ladies became his wife.

Salimo's was soon caught up in similar incidents involving his other friends; in this case, the friend was informed by his girlfriend that she was going to go for a weekend to work on a business plan, now that she was a consultant. But unknown to her, one of the Joes' group competitors informed Salimo's friend, "What business plan? They're off to Seychelles to go for a weekend with her boss."

So, without hesitation, Harun enlisted the company of Salimo to go on to retrieve some of his precious items that he has lent to the girlfriend. Unexpectedly, Harun and Salimo arrived at the flat of the lady and caught them at a moment when they were loading things into their car, obviously going off to safari. This lady was later named *Kaptula* lady! *Kaptula* because she liked wearing shorts, which was not common among women in the country.

So, on arrival, the last items were being loaded into the car, and these were the mountain bikes, and fortunately, these mountain bikes had been given as gifts to this lady by Harun, and Harun could not avoid noticing that those precious gifts of his were not only being taken away for a holiday, but one of the beneficiaries was going to be his competitor. Harun demanded immediately to have the bicycles back, as she no longer was entitled to these gifts.

No amount of persuasion from the lady could make Harun change his mind. So, at long last, he let both ladies go and Salimo was given the responsibility to dismantle the bicycles and put them in the boot of the car. The next thing that Harun demanded was access to the flats so he could take away his clothes, and secondly, the key to the car that he had given to the young lady. To avoid embarrassment, the young lady decided to comply, and so she led him into the house. He picked up his neatly hung suits. He put them in the car and took the bicycle which Salimo had finished dismantling, and put them in the car.

Well, for some reason not quite known to anybody, the lady was happy with him and saying that at the very least, he should let her have the bicycles. She would later at least use them that weekend.

But Harun was adamant, eventually telling her, "Your friend can buy you bicycles."

Having to retrieve the bicycles and all these things, and having the key to their car that he had given to that lady, he and Salimo then left. Salimo was driving the car they came in and Harun was driving the car that was with the lady previously. That was the end of a short-lived relationship, but not before Ole Naimara challenged him as to what he was up to. Salimo was sure that the fact that things had become too expensive in the project, they were completing the project of building the hospital, and Naimara was complaining that the expense was too much. Things were over-inflated, and now Naimara said "I understand why things are getting more and more expensive. With this *Kaptula* lady, I don't expect you to be working hard." The *Kaptula* lady went and that was the last time she was ever seen at the school.

***

August 1982 marked a turning point for many in the country and also for the country in general. At the macro level it was a wake-up call for Arap Moi and his government and his general demeanour and relationship with the people changed forever from one of fraternisation to one of mistrust and the need to exercise a heavy hand. At the micro level or rather at the personal level, this was also a turning point for Salimo.

What went wrong? What had happened to bring these changes of great magnitude in the country? The single event that happened suddenly like a typhoon or an earthquake without warning, without expectation was a morning announcement that Moi's government had been overthrown. A group of Air Force officers stormed the national broadcaster to cover the institution and commenced a repeated message to the nation to the effect that the corrupt and inept government of Arap Moi had been overthrown and that the military was in control and that everybody should remain calm.

Unlike other military coups that had happened on the continent, this particular one did have a unique feature to itself at the national broadcaster, which was the only outlet for news. There was pop music being played. One could have expected martial or low music or military nature music but in this case there was an abundance of pop music from all the artists in the country and from abroad. It was different whereas it was supposed to be a grave mood in the nation. Nevertheless, the only source of information and news continued to play the high life kind of music, probably indicating that the new rulers wanted a better Kenya, a Kenya where everybody enjoyed music at liberty.

At the personal level this set into motion events in the lives of many people, particularly Salimo. It set into motion a chain of events that led to the eventual marriage to his sweetheart. For Salimo and others it was a normal weekend. They had gone out until late in the night and being late or by design the young student did not go back to school or to the halls of residence. She proceeded home to her future home to spend the rest of the weekend.

May be as a result of the festivities of the night it wasn't until late Sunday morning when the couple could detect sporadic light firearm noise from the city. "Did you hear that? Yes, sounds like fireworks." With that the couple went back to sleep but shortly thereafter the butler in the house arrived and knocked loudly to say there was trouble in the city and they needed to open the radio and check what was going on.

From a normal weekend, Sunday morning turned out to be a day of high tension, expectation and uncertainty. No information was forthcoming, except periodically the news would be stopped and strange announcements would be proclaimed, for example the army or the police had been disbanded and the police officers were required to lay down weapons and evacuate government premises and the offices.

As the day wore on and the pop music continued, suddenly at around one o'clock the familiar voice of the announcer usually associated with the popular program that aimed to discourage people from and quote and ill-mannered behaviour in Swahili generally known as, '*je, huu ni ungwana*' which literally meant, is this gentleman behaviour, is this civilised behaviour? Yes more, is this civilised behaviour? Then he went on to narrate some sordid event and behaviour that needed to be condemned. Leonard Mambo was the anchor who was associated with this program.

Around about one o'clock he came on the air and amid some light weapons going off in the background he announced, "This was rubbish, *upusi, upusi mingi*. This was absolute nonsense and rubbish. The government is back in power. I'm here at the national broadcasting station and together with me is General Mohamed and I can assure you that everything is back in order." Obviously in this confused state, it was unclear whether this was fiction or true or whether there was another one of these unexpected events.

However by late evening Arap Moi appeared on the air and announced that the disturbances by the Air Force had been contained and that everything was back in order and Kenyans should go around their life without influence. However, the announcement also said people should avoid the city centre in the city of Nairobi. By the end of the week it was clear that to a large extent this was a city centre disturbance and the barracks that are located in the city centre and that the general state were still confused, there was not sufficient information forthcoming to tell Kenyans what had happened and how it had been contained.

For the people in the city of Nairobi including Salimo, normal life did not come back immediately. Indeed, very soon it was clear that they would remain indoor for the good part of the week. There was a semi-curfew in place. By the next morning, mid-morning Monday, the hot spots of the disturbance had been identified to include the University of Nairobi. An announcement from the office of the vice chancellor informed students that the university had been closed indefinitely and students were given until 6:00 PM to collect their belongings, pack and leave the hostels. The task statement said, "Hall of residence could be closed immediately at 6:00 PM"

It was at this moment that Salimo and his future wife realised how serious matters were. Reluctantly they agreed to drive to the ladies hostel so she could collect her belongings and wait for further orders. The two kilometres to the hostel took about 30 minutes to clear. Not because of traffic but because of the many roadblocks and checkpoints by the police who wanted to be sure those going through were not criminals. The seriousness of the circumstances unfolded when Salimo and his sweetheart arrived at the halls of residency and noted something strange which turned out to be the female students being frogmarched into their halls of residence. About 100 metres away was the last point where cars were allowed and once the occupants or the students went out, they joined a queue of counterparts on their fours being frogmarched into the hostel.

As 6:00 PM approached, Salimo grew restless and unsure about what would happen and not sure whether to go back, having being rattled by the many roadblocks and checkpoints and the menacing manner of the army units that were manning the checkpoints. He nevertheless considered his responsibility and duty to go back and retrace his steps to the box if possible to collect his sweetheart. It was feared that from past experience during those disturbances the military people found an excuse to engage in all forms of ugliest impudent undressing and rape. With great fear, Salim drove towards the box to collect his sweetheart.

To his relief, one kilometre from his house, he met his sweetheart in a great hurry in the company of other friends. Everybody was relieved to be united. The group, Salimo, his sweetheart and two other friends then retreated to the sanctuary of his flat to observe events from a distance. Everything was peaceful and quiet but gradually the stores were closing down.

The supermarkets were closed for most of the time or it wasn't unclear how safe it was to go into the city to replenish.

It's surprising to know the city dwellers are at the mercy of the people from the villages who normally stock the supplies, it would appear, on a daily basis. Any disturbance of one day or more will result in depletion of stores and essentially whole population in the cities could starve to death. During the week there had been many rumours from the newspapers and from external news outlets indicating that the hunt was on for the perpetrators of this uprising and that many people were being arrested or had been arrested and that people were being shot indiscriminately in the city centre and people were not being allowed to go into the city.

Looking back, one can appreciate the technological revolution that has taken place that it is possible for communication to go on even in the midst of such a disturbance using cellular phones but in those days everything would come to a complete halt. No communication, no information, everybody was hoping for the best. As the week wore off, the information started to filter through slowly and life started to return to normality in the city but there were disturbing rumours that students who were leaving to their homes were being pulled out of the public transport vehicles, buses and other means because the university had been identified as a collaborator with the uprising.

Indeed this was based on the fact that at the time of initial announcement of the coup by the military officers, the student leader was in their company and the student leader went on a tirade of condemnation of the corrupt and unpopular regime of Arap Moi. With that, the security forces concluded that this uprising had something to do with the university students. Indeed, university students were always associated with any unpopular activity against the government.

These tidbits of information regarding the mistreatment or maltreatment of students as they went home were unconfirmed and probably to a large extent unfounded. However, as said before, during this time it was impossible to know, it was like people were living in the dark ages where communication was by mouth to mouth or written newspaper and what the newspaper said was the very truth. At the end of the week Salimo ventured into the streets to go and replenish the stores from the supermarket and also to be in touch with colleagues.

Fortunately, being a doctor, it was always possible to identify yourself as one and as part of going to the hospital to deal with emergencies, also replenish your stores. At the hospital it was a tale of horror. There are many people with gunshot injuries and there were now reported to be people missing. Hospitals were stretched but they could cope with the numbers. Although the event had taken place in the middle of the city, it had happened during the weekend and there had been no confrontation between protagonists and the Air Force which had caused the disturbance.

Indeed the only skirmishes occurred on that very day of Sunday and it was during the fight to liberate the national broadcasting station. Thereafter, it was more of a mopping up operation and rounding up of Air Force officers to ensure that there were no pockets of resistance or that the system would not be surprised by another uprising. As the week wore on, information indicated that the guards from the far west were able to link up with Arap Moi and drive in a huge convoy into the city.

Later it would emerge that Arap Moi, unsure of what to do, had been rescued by his own security men as he was in the village and they had driven him to unknown place in a private car and were monitoring the situation by a relay of informants. At a certain moment in time when he was informed that all was clear he came out of the woods to join the contingent that led him to the city. Whether they did not trust airlifting him in a helicopter, nobody knows but it is known that there was a huge convoy for military vehicles, at the centre of which was Arap Moi, being driven to the city.

Later on there was also news that Arap Moi himself was not sure what he was to expect when he arrived in the city. From moment to moment he kept inquiring from his handlers whether it was safe to go back to the city, particularly when he could hear some gunshots in the distance. Those driving him to the city never informed him; sometimes they were firing to scare off onlookers and to ensure that nobody was injured as they went to the city.

As normality descended on the city and people started going around their businesses, then people started to take stock of whose relative was missing, whose relative was in the Air Force, and where they were. The government also started putting out some statistics, which to a large extent are highly distributed. The news claimed that, no more than 200 people lost their lives but other sources indicated that there were probably more people who died.

Indeed Otis and Sagini were now out looking for their relatives who had been officers in the Air Force. Salimo and Sagini would later in the week, no, later in the month learn that Sagini's brother was in one of the revulsive prisons at Shimoni. But this happened after Salimo had taken his sweetheart and escorted her to her rural home to an unorthodox entry into the family. It was unorthodox because he was not expected. Normally that's now not how a man will announce his intentions to get married into a family.

His arrival therefore caused a bit of a stir in the household. Whereas everybody was jubilant that their daughter had arrived, they were rather disturbed that for the first time she arrived home in the company of a man unknown to them, a stranger. One who was, moreover, from another ethnic group. Indeed his future father-in-law required six to eight hours to steam off his anger and displeasure and to ease these unexpected turn of events. Anyway, that set in motion an unstoppable train of events that ended with a wedding.

Towards the conclusion of this disturbance each of the Joes had a tale to relate. Otis, in the company of Sagini, had gone to Kamiti, the maximum-security prison in the country to look for one of his cousins who was a member of the Air Force. After going from office to office, he was informed that the young man would be facing the military court, the court martial and therefore they should stop visiting him or worrying, they would be informed. Sagini learned that his brother was detained at Shimo la Tewa at the coast and that gradually restrictions were being removed and relatives could visit and talk to these unfortunate officers.

Salim and Sagini travelled one morning to the coast in a bus to Shimo la Tewa prison to find out whether his brother was actually there or it was just a fabrication. For them it was the first time to visit anybody in a maximum-security prison. They registered with the desk and they were given time to wait so that they could talk to the officer. At a point in time they were told, "You have been given 15 minutes to talk to your loved ones. Leave all your belongings here and talk to them for 15 minutes."

To the shock of both visitors, they thought they were going to have an occasion to hug this long-lost brother, only to realise that it was like a chicken pen with openings where prisoners would be on the other side of the wall and the relatives on this side, in more or less a common hall and both parties would be shouting loudly to be heard because everybody was trying to deliver one message or the other or to express great joy that they could see each other. This hullabaloo went on for precisely 15 minutes.

At the end of the 15 minutes, the guard appeared and ordered everything to come to an end. The prisoners retreated and the relatives retreated to their own side. All this happened in such a brief moment and for most relatives the only other thing they could do it was to pass on to the prisoner a couple of bucks to use for their upkeep because it was rumoured that in this prison, the level of care was so wanting that if you didn't have your own resources to both bribe the guards to buy good food for you, you could die not so much from starvation but your energy reserves and body build would be so reduced that your immune system would also fail.

Indeed many prisoners ended up having tuberculosis from which they died subsequently. Sagini was able to hand to his brother 100 bob which is what he could safely deliver through the little opening in the window. At the national level Arap Moi's government embarked on a major crackdown and clean-up operation. The Air Force was disbanded. This was despite the fact that this was a constitutionally mandated arm of security. It was yet to be recreated in a new name.

For those in power for the first time they realised how perilous it is to hang on to power and that overnight, things can change and therefore one had to be prepared, as the crackdown continued, particularly aimed at the military. As detentions also were being declared for the civilians who were working with the military, those in power for the first time were also planning for potentially an unexpected exit. As happens when there's this level of insecurity, the old system changed into how to ensure that when out of power one did not succumb to poverty and suffering. Hence started an era of looting and plunder of national assets.

The goodwill of the first four years of Moi's government had been brought to it is knees by this single event. This uprising was the first of its kind in the country. Indeed that time Kenya was described as an island of peace because, of all the British colonies, Kenya was one of the few countries that had not been visited by a military coup. For this event to happen was a major shock and a turning point in the history of the nation.

To Moi it was a wake-up call that the public is not to be trusted; the people were not to be trusted. They can turn against you at the most unexpected time. Therefore he had to protect himself against any such eventuality. One way of doing it was to ensure that those who are entrusted with the security of the nation and his own security on the survival were well rewarded. Those around him realised that one had to eat while the weighing was good and therefore there was a major push to identify what could be plundered or looted to the advantage of the looters in the government.

Government property was being auctioned or allocated at more or less throwaway prices. Military officers were being rewarded more, for government was buying their allegiance by allocating them land and plots in prime areas of the city. This went on until the country was almost at its knees at the height of the grand corruption known as Goldenberg. Goldenberg was a great scam that had been orchestrated by one Kamlesh Pattni, a shrewd businessman of Asian extraction who had identified loopholes in the economic system and exploited it with impunity.

He masterminded a scheme called export compensation where those who exported raw materials or exported to the benefits of the nation would get a 35% waiver on their tax. Indeed for the first time it was recorded that Kenya was a major gold exporter despite there being no known goldmine of commercial proportion. The use of gold as the element for smuggling and earning this export compensation had a secondary effect, that was of devaluation of the Kenya shilling. Inflation went high and the Kenya shilling became extremely weak against all other currencies.

At the height of the Goldenberg scam, infant mortality which had gone down to 60, gradually started to spiral out of control. Neonatal mortality started to rise. All socio-economic indicators in the country started to regress. In short, all the gain that had been made during Jomo Kenyatta's time and part of Moi's time started to be lost and the economy started to shrink but it will appear that the economy of a stable nation cannot be exhausted overnight. Therefore, instead of Moi being the passing cloud that had been described when he took over power in 1978, he ended up being the longest-serving president Kenya will ever have, with almost 22 years in power.

Moi outlived all predictions. The only prediction that came true is by Jomo Kenyatta himself. Jomo Kenyatta had described Moi as the giraffe with a long neck who sees far. Moi himself in due course had described himself as a professor of medicine, as professor of politics. That there is very little anybody else could teach him in politics. He was rude and indeed even long after he had lost power he continued to turn the wheels of power behind the scenes. Indeed, as late as 2007 when there was the great political crash in Kenya, Moi would say, "Bad politics, bad life. *Siasa mbaya, maisha mbaya*." That's what he would say; that one needed to be more than just a president to lead a nation.

The causes of the attempted coup in 1982 August will never be known for sure. Word is clear that it was the junior officers in the Air Force, therefore the Air Force generally in the country was regarded as the elite arm of the three arms of the military. It had people who had gone to school more than their compatriots and they prided themselves on flying high. The Air Force was also to a large extent manned by quite a few people from one ethnic group that was heavily linked to the opposition groups in Kenya, particularly the short lived KPU; Kenya People's Union which was engineered by the first vice president of Kenya, Oginga Odinga himself.

How many people died during this short-lived disturbance? Nobody knows. However, for the first time in Kenya there was a court martial and a number of these mis-adventurers, as one would say, were sentenced to death. Indeed this was the only time that military officers had been condemned to death and the sentences had been carried out. Later on, talking to friends and relatives in the village, Salimo learnt that the people saw this as an attempt by the young officers to enrich themselves or to get themselves into power.

"You know these guys tried to milk the cow before tying the legs". This was the main perception in the village. That the officers, having realised that power had some trappings, wanted also to have a piece of the action but were ill-prepared to cling onto power. Normally when people in the village are milking a cow they will release the calf and when the calf is enjoying with the mother cow they'll tie the hind legs with a rope and then the calf can be withdrawn safely and the milkman goes into action.

In this case the analogy which was being given is that this ill advice related to the officers who were impatient. They wanted to milk before tying the cow securely. When you do that, the cow throws a kick and anybody on its way will be injured. In fact one old man put it very succinctly when he narrated the event. He said, "Oh you know, my son is in Shimo la Tewa. He was part of that group of officers who were trying to milk the cow and when it threw out the kick he caught it right on his cheek. But luckily he's alive and we hope one day he will be released."

Otis and his colleagues went now to check on their relative who had been condemned to death by the court martial. After several inquiries at Kamiti nobody seemed to know this individual but when they mentioned the other names, the officer with a giggle in his voice said, "Oh you mean 'ile' condemned?" He said, "Yes." Meaning, as they learnt later, that once you are condemned to death even your name changes to "the condemned". The guards and everybody in prison no longer regard you as being alive because you have already been condemned to death. You are only waiting for your day.

We would have saved ourselves a lot of time and energy if we had gone there and said, we have come to see and bid farewell to our condemned compatriots. Once you informed them that they were those who were waiting to be hanged; the condemned, then they'd quickly go to the list of the condemned and they would tell you where your loved one was. With Sagini a regular visit to Shimo la Tewa became routine for two years before his brother could be released and go home to his newly wedded wife. He was only too happy to learn that while he was in prison the brothers and the rest had continued to ensure that the process that he had started of marriage proceeded and the dowry had been paid and his wife was safely at home.

The military leader who declared himself the third president of Kenya had joined the long list of the condemned. He had tried to commandeer one of the Air Force planes into Tanzania and unfortunately the good relations between the two countries did not augur well for him. Within a few weeks, the two governments had worked out a deportation order and he was repatriated back into the country to face the music, as Moi would say.

On his part, Moi continued to fortify himself against any such uprising. The secret police was enhanced and any pockets of opposition would be detected very early and action taken. A new wave of detentions and arrests ensued. This was to be followed by a countermeasure once more saying, for every action there is an equal action in the opposite direction. The more Arap Moi detained people, the more his people were tortured in his torture chambers; one of them was right in the centre of the city in a building called Nyayo building. The more people got disgruntled, the more they pushed for change.

It didn't take long for the opposition to start mobilizing and it didn't take long for a multiparty movement to emerge, but that's a story for another day. For now, Arap Moi had survived the greatest challenge to his power. He had survived with his life and none of his ministers or senior officers had been affected. For the university, this transformed the institution fundamentally. The politically charged atmosphere was diffused almost for eternity. For people like Salimo and others the events that this political typhoon set into motion were irreversible.

A nation is only a nation for the moment there's peace and tranquillity. The moment peace and tranquillity goes, the nation ceases to exist. Indeed, as Jimmy would say later on, the poor people have no use for rich people but the rich people have need for the poor. They serve them, they work for them, they buy from them. Therefore, he could say, it is important for the rich to invest in the welfare of the poor. It's what he came to describe as investing in social order.

***

One of the responsibilities of a registrar in the department of surgery was to spend at least three months as the casualty officer. What this meant was that he or she would be managing hot emergencies as they arrived at the casualty of the hospital. He'd conduct the triage, determine who needed immediate attention and effectively distribute the casualties so that the effective and comprehensive care could be given, which was appropriate with respect to the level of injury. As the casualty officer, Salimo was required to ensure the smooth operations of the entire department as often patients came with a range of presentations from coma to raucous patients who obviously had had too much before they were clobbered or they were hurt in an accident. Often, Salimo would spend the whole night sitting on the casualty chair, luckily the institution provided for some light refreshment in coffee and tea. There was no provision for a resting room or bed to relax in. On the rare quiet nights, Salimo would spend a good part of the night in his car reclining on the seat, with instructions to the nurse on duty to call him once there was an emergency.

This was not the case during month-ends. At month end, the place was like a disaster zone. There would be a mix of people with all manners of problems. Some in coma through alcohol overindulgence, some with cuts through violent confrontations after a busy night of binge drinking, or purely from road accidents. For the casualty officer, it required quick action and response to quickly differentiate those who were in immediate danger of death or gross complications out of the injury, determine who needed to go to theatre directly, who needed to go to for a further investigation, which was usually a plain x-ray. He'd also be required to merely say who would do with a good dose of glucose to bring them out of their alcoholic coma. In this station, all the skills required for basic life support, advanced cardiac support and trauma and injury management would be called into action as often, it would be difficult to find the senior colleagues to lend a hand. The casualty officer would sometimes be required to proceed to theatre in case of a life-threatening situation.

For the city of Nairobi, life at the casualty department was predictable. The full range of what could be expected on an average evening could easily be predicted. Hardly was the casualty officer confronted with such event as a terrorist bomb having exploded. Yet this is what happened on one of those busy and unexpected events in the city. Extending hostilities across oceans and borders, terrorists in pursuit of Israelis had struck the Norfolk Hotel, a popular and high class spot in the middle of the city, situated not too far from the University of Nairobi and also from a spot, which Naimara claims would be the take-off point when people go to Heaven. According to Naimara, this spot is housed in a synagogue at the centre of the city, close to Uhuru Highway. The announcement over the radio indicated that the bomb had gone off in early hours of the evening and that there were many casualties.

Fortunately for Salimo, the clientele who patronised Norfolk Hotel were not the kind who would seek care or attention in a public facility. Most of them were quickly shepherded through the many private hospitals in the city where they could receive care and attention not available to the ordinary *mwananchi*, which is the common man, in the country. Only when these facilities were overwhelmed did they seek assistance from the public national hospital. The overflow of patients to the public hospital only started arriving later in the night. This event marked a turning point in the history of the country, particularly the initiation into the hostile world out there. It is a tragic relic of the cold war where Kenya was perceived as allied to the USA and, by extension, to Israel and that Kenya continued to entertain business enterprises from both Israel and the USA. Therefore, for this reason, everybody and anybody in the country should suffer the consequences.

Until now, Kenya had only rare such events of exploding bombs. If a bomb exploded, it was likely to be a device originating from the Second World War deep in the farms, or in the forest. Kenya was only engaged in a prolonged or protracted fight for cessation by what the colonial government described as the North Frontier District. This is the district that borders Somalia. Ethnic groups of Somali origin had been fomenting rebellion through explosions of landmines, ambushes of public transport vehicles and government restorations. From there on, Kenya was exposed to the risk of international terrorist attacks. Not even the umbrella of security systems extended by the US and other governments would ensure that the country was immune to tragic events like these. Kenya was now at the centre of the international stage with respect to terrorist attacks. Given the earlier preparatory processes as an intern, the transition into and out of postgraduate was like a walk in the park for Salimo and his friends.

Indeed, at this time most of them started to get organised. Organised meant transitioning from unmarried bachelors into a married adult life. One by one, in different ways, each of them entered matrimonial relationships. Some through come-we-stay, others through a wedding ceremony and others through simply a walk-in.

Joe held that usually marriage is an event that is determined by the woman. It is the woman who decides the moment she wants to get married and must remain on the driving seat of the process. From time to time when confronted with the issue he would say, "Well, she has not decided." Unfortunately for him, one day two ladies decided that they were going to get married to him, both of them on the same day. When asked what he was going to do to resolve this dilemma, he characteristically came with an answer nobody could dispute. "Well, I have decided not to decide."

He was pursued with, "What do you mean you have decided not to decide?"

"Well," he explained, "Well, a problem or a situation arises, one can take active measures to define the way forward about how to make the decision. Two, or one can decided to let events take their own course. That's deciding not to decide. In this case, I'll let the women sort it out themselves." Well, luckily for him, the women sorted it out themselves when one of them decided this was not worth fighting for.

The remaining woman just walked in and stayed and declared herself his wife. No amount of entreating her to exit or to make a more planned event would convince her. Indeed, one such attempt elicited the response, "You, where have you held in store a suitable husband for me to leave this one and go for that one?" With those emphatic words, she stayed, never to leave again. As for Joe, in the company of Salimo, he went and registered at the office of the registrar or the Attorney General's office and they went to town and had a drink and that was the end. Salimo opted to go the long way and ended up with a church ceremony. All in all, by the end of the postgraduate training, the

Joe group had moved on from being young professionals into mature adults and medical specialists.

Incidentally, one of the Joes had his marriage arranged. Once he went out to serve in the rural community, the village people not wanting to see their esteemed doctor walking to the kiosk to buy provisions and spending time making lunch for himself or dinner for himself, identified a suitable companion. They ensconced that companion into the residency of the doctor and she stayed and was happily married from thence ever more. Ben never stops admiring this young doctor for his bravery. To him, he represented the ultimate of humanity and the understanding of what marriage is.

If one was to summarise the three or four years of medical specialisation with respect to Salimo, one would say he came, he participated, he gained more experience and knowledge, and he left an accomplished surgeon; ready to go to the field and practice his skills in line with modern surgical practices. Did it meet the standard Professor Mohanji had set; that it would be highly manual and that the level of intellect required would be lower than that of a psychiatrist or that of a physician? No. At this stage, the surgeons, in an attempt to elevate the profession, had declared that a surgical specialist is a physician who can also carry out surgical operations. In other words, a surgeon must be an accomplished internist and a proficient hands-on person. Indeed, according to Terry, the surgeon needs to insure the whole hand while the obstetrician needed to insure his two fingers. Even more accurately, the surgeon needed to insure the index finger while the obstetrician needs to insure the index and the middle finger. These are the tools of the operation.

In the words of the Swahili saying, the legs of the hyena are also its tools for survival – "*Mguu wa nyang'au ni chembe lake*".

***

The concept of time is relative. Their medical specialisation came to a rather sudden end, or so they thought. They did not realise that they had actually only been at it for the past four years, including one lost during the fateful attempted coup in Kenya. Once more, the Joe group was distributed, and soon they were dispatched to various locations only accessible on a regular basis by a fixed telephone. This was before the time of mobile phones. Comfortably seated in this new location some wasted no time to put a stamp on the surgical services of this district. This was a medium-sized district, population 500,000, with about 300 healthcare workers. No sooner had they settled to start the surgical practice than the medical officer left to go and do some other training, and so, Simon was immediately handed additional responsibilities of the management and administration of the district healthcare services.

This is something that he had not been prepared for. Hardly anybody was prepared for this kind of assignment during that time. The responsibility was conferred on the oldest or the most qualified doctor in the institution. It was naturally assumed that, in the healthcare system, the doctor is the head of the team. It was while serving in this capacity, that Salimo encountered the first real case of HIV/AIDS. The patient had come, and registered for antenatal care, but appeared to be not too far from labour. Jenyuwa, the patient, was advised to come back when the labour had started, as was the practice. Little did the nurses know, that this particular patient had migrated to the coast of the country, in search of greener pastures. On coming back, the rumour had preceded her, that she was carrying that dreaded disease.

Now, in the settlement area, where cultural sensitivities and practices had all but disappeared, she was not welcome, not even to her parents' home. Not that the parents did not want her, but the neighbours were adamant that having someone with that kind of infection posed a major risk to all the men, young and old alike, in the village. Therefore, she was not welcome to their community. Now, late in the evening, she reappeared at the hospital labour ward, and a new crew was on duty, and the delivery was conducted successfully. The mother and child were put in the bed together, as was the routine, because that's the only way of keeping the infant warm in those days. The next day, she was discharged with a baby, both of them looking healthy and bubbling.

Salimo was summoned back to the hospital two days later, because a baby had been found abandoned in the city. As there were no known parents, the local administration wanted the baby taken care of at the hospital. There was no good reason to deny this request, so the baby was admitted, and put under the care of the nursing staff. As time went by, there was always a lingering suspicion that this baby might be the baby born by the same mother who had been ostracised by her parents and her community, and now had abandoned the baby. Those days, there was very little known about HIV/AIDS. Indeed, the teaching was that this was a scourge, visiting upon people with alternative sex practices; particularly anal sex, and more so, homosexuals. That was the standard teaching at this stage. Curiosity having been aroused, Salimo decided to try and assess the extent to which this new disease, as it was known, had extended, or spread, into these rural districts. Therefore, together with a colleague from Denmark, young Dr Sagini and Simon embarked on a community-wide survey, targeting school-aged, sexually active boys and girls.

Indeed, after what could have been considered a very large sample at that stage, of about 2,000 young people, there were only less than five who could fit the bill of having signs and symptoms of HIV. Indeed, it was a negligible number, even after the same samples were tested by the more sophisticated method, which was then the Western blot. Until that time it was only known that it affected only people with alternative sex, and these people were those who had been influenced by other cultures. The finger was being pointed at tourists and foreigners. Having to assure themselves that HIV/AIDS was not a public health problem, or at least it did not exist in such alarming proportions, it was agreed there was no need to worry too much, but to be careful, particularly in one's sexual habits or partners. Like any district hospitals in the republic then, these institutions were beleaguered by shortages of all kinds, whether it be the clean linen, pharmaceuticals or human resources. The facilities were particularly worrisome.

Indeed, Salimo's theatre, although new, always had one problem or the other, particularly their operation theatre lights. This is where in this district Simon learned the art and science of improvisation. Therefore, the frequent burned out bulbs, which were also extremely expensive to replace, and there being no maintenance budget, it was always impossible to have the theatre lights working all the time. One way of improvising a solution to this was to use fluorescent tubes mounted on an equilateral triangle, and having two sets of these tubes in parallel, so a smaller set inside the triangle, and a longer set just at the edge of the triangle, both of them controlled by different switches. Also, the board mounting them could be lifted higher to make it cooler or brought down if more light was needed. Alternatively, if more light was needed, both sets of lights; the inner triangle and the outer triangle, would be switched on, but where there was no need for additional light, then only the outer set was used. This innovation lasted no less than 20 years before the properly manufactured theatre light could be mounted.

At this stage the electricity was stable enough so as to not blow the bulbs as frequently as it used to in the past. Needless to say, by this time many patients had benefited from this improvisation. The second time of improvisation that was introduced was to overcome the senseless loss of patient because there were no intravenous fluids. Now that they also had a qualified degree holder pharmacist together with Simon, they contrived the idea of making their own saline and 5% extras, and even local anaesthetics injectable, mixing at least. The only thing harder was to procure and own a machine that could safely cork and de-cork bottles that are used for these intravenous fluids. Soon such a machine was procured from far lands of Italy and pretty soon the hospital was making its own life-saving fluids. The cost plummeted to less than 10% of what it was costing the hospital. For the first time, for one year running, this hospital did not have a debt to pay in town for fluids which were borrowed or taken on loan to save patients.

This improvisation proved that it was possible in at least a low resource setting to create a healthcare system that served a wide section of the community, or life-threatening conditions could be managed using improvised methodologies. As a district medical officer, Simon was also serving as the public office in charge of the public health aspects of the district. Therefore, it included inspection of premises they used for eating, lodging, schools, places of worship, and a place which was used for public convenience. Why it became necessary to call them district medical officer of health is beyond comprehension. One would have thought that medical and health served the same purpose, however the holders of this post did not want to be called district health officers. They wanted to be called district medical officers, DMOs. It was while serving in this capacity that Salimo encountered many endemics, particularly cholera, water-bound epidemics, cholera and malaria. These were brand new as water was usually available from shallow wells, or rivers which were used by human beings, wild animals, and also domestic animals.

Indeed in the community it was always held true that one had to be very mean to deny anybody, including a stranger, a drink of water. Normally they would say, "Why would we withhold this free gift which even the hyena enjoys for free?" Preventing these endemics was extremely difficult, but Salimo and his team were prepared to try their best. They conjured the idea of a total enumeration of all the inhabitants of the district subdivided into smaller units and assigning public health officers into each of these units, either at the village level or sub-location level; usually for anything up to 2000 inhabitants. Fortunately the country had produced a lot of these public health officers and they had been deployed mainly to inspect meat. The team was determined to take away that responsibility of inspection of meat from this very useful cadre. Indeed often it would be that the lady or gentlemen would be working generally from his home, or her home; would go to the marketplace early in the morning when the butcher was slaughtering; to inspect the meat. They will be given a pound of flesh of all their troubles.

The institution did not always provide transport or travel allowance, and so they made a beef about it. This exercise of enumeration and repeated visits to look at their hygiene, at waste management and disposal, at general cleanliness, the use of water, and the use of food and nutrition, proved very popular and very much welcome by the community. It was in this district that Salimo was confronted by the politics of the day. The local Member of Parliament was a minister in Jomo Kenyatta's government, but he was the only one with the audacity to vote against the government which had resolved to merely note the report of the commission of inquiry into the disappearance and death of Josiah Mwang Kariuki, or JM as he was popularly known. Not surprisingly, retribution from Jomo Kenyatta was instant. He was relieved of his ministerial duties with immediate effect. Now freed from officialdom, Masinde Muliro continued agitating for better conditions for social charities, justice, equality, and against corruption. That did not endear him to the government of the day. Now, as elections were nearing, the district commissioner was a member of a cadre that prided themselves as having been dispatched and appointed by the office of the president.

They claimed they represented the super ministry; that they were in charge of other ministries and other operations and procuring security. Therefore, from time to time they would be used or misused to abuse the power that they owned together with the chiefs. Masinde was making too much noise in the neighbourhood and he was making the government uncomfortable. The local district commissioner approached the DMO and requested him to do something to silence this rogue politician, which he was considered. What could Salimo do to support the government of the day? The commissioner advised that one way is helping economically. Therefore, he advised Salimo to close the two-star hotel in the city that this politician, at the onset of independence, had acquired from the foreign masters. It was in itself an icon of independence. He said that most of these politicians had easy access to what could have been, ill-gotten wealth. He was not a businessman. It was simpler, since they made it. There was a rumour that you might encounter a team of cockroaches in the bedrooms, or even rats. Nobody had really ever seen this vermin in this hotel. The idea was for the district medical officer to condemn this hotel and close it on health grounds.

Unknown to him, Salimo was also endeared to the idea of social justice and found this scheme against his principles, so the commissioner dropped the idea all together. For Salimo, there was still another reason why he dropped it, because as a result of the perennial shortages of drugs, finances for maintenance and even cleaning the compound of the hospital, one visiting the institution never failed to notice the long-beaked birds enjoying a feast on human tissues, particularly placentas. In the particular corner where the pits were overflowing with waste as there being no system for incineration, the smell was always pervasive. For Salimo to try and close the hotel for the fact that there might be rats or cockroaches would be fodder for Masinde, who would question why they were supposed to remain closed. From time to time they would say they must get rid of these things which were making the hospital look a laughing stock.

While a district surgeon and the manager at the same time, Salimo's training was put to the extreme test. For example it was not uncommon for a diagnosis to be made and the patient referred to the central hospital, as the practice of medicine required. Also it was equally not uncommon for the patients to decline surgical referral; the main reason being that when a patient from the rural areas is admitted, it's the whole village which is admitted. There would be a steady stream of visitors to keep an eye on their loved ones. Transferring a patient to 500 kilometres away, or 300 kilometres away was in itself a barrier to this social interaction. The whole system was not culturally sensitive. From time to time Simon would be doing procedures that would naturally require a high calibre hospital, a highly trained anaesthetist, and to some extent some intensive care observations.

The human being is a well-made machine, self-healing, and self-perpetrating, so to say. With minimum care and the best surgical skills, the outcome in this small rural facility was no worse than what you'd get in a centralised hospital, which often also has the disadvantage of attracting some of the most drug-resistant bugs. The best day for Salimo in this facility was Thursday when he would drive himself to neighbouring districts – they did not have a surgeon – and perform surgery on patients who were not admitted by the medical assistants or the medical officers and would have otherwise been referred. This was a source of fulfilment for the surgeon as well as the inhabitants in these far-off districts. It was while serving in this capacity that one night Salimo was summoned to a remote hospital 100 miles away, to go and assist in saving the life of a patient. The trip to and from Salimo's residence took easily four hours. Fortunately for the patient the anaesthetic which was used was a facial mask with a light anaesthesia and at that stage it was ether.

Within 15-20 minutes of arrival, the repair of the uterus was complete, for that was what caused the problem. It was an obstetric labour, a ruptured uterus and a complicated caesarean section by the assessment of the doctor. On this charge, both the patient and the primary doctor were very happy that surprisingly the mother and child were alive and healthy; thanks to the mission of the ladies who had conjured the idea of linking their hospital to the hospital where there was the only surgeon available. The nursing sisters at this facility never stopped to express their immense gratitude for the support they continued to get from the facility where Salimo was a resident. Indeed they never failed to reciprocate in kind. This happened seven years later, when Salimo, needing asylum from bandits and the elements, would need resuscitation and thereafter would benefit from the long comradeship that he courted with these Catholic nuns. It was while also at this particular hospital that Salimo learned that sometimes people who are considered by society as insane are just like drunk people: the most honest people you can come across.

There was one Monda, for example, who was not violent, was not quite mentally inline as it was described, but he never bothered anybody, but from time to time he caused embarrassment, or he caused some solution to be found in the village, based on how one looked at it. Occasionally, Monda would invade the church and go to the pulpit and request to say something as a God-fearing person. It was on one of these occasions that he arrived and announced that he had an important message to deliver. Not wanting to upset him and upset the whole program, the pastor allowed him to make his announcement and he was advised to make it brief. Then Monda proceeded to produce a foolscap where he had list of the people from the village for whom he had received communication from heavens indicating that he needed to deliver the message. The message was that in this church, there were people who will go to heaven, and there are people who will remain on earth, and there were people who would go to the everlasting fire, the residency of the devil.

He then took the list and started naming one after another, for the ones who will go to heaven he would read: "So and so, yes." He would put a tick against the name and point to heaven; so and so who was considered not to be too religious he would read and put it under his armpit and state: "This one no, no, no this one there are many question marks". On and on Monda called out the names, much to the great amusement of everybody in church. At the end of the exercise they thanked him profusely and he left without any commotion. Needless to say some of those names that he held in check and said needed to be scrutinised as they might not go to heaven, were some of the prominent members of the church; even the community and the village had questions about their performance. Indeed one of those ones who were named as not headed heavenward was one who the people claimed was pinching the tithes and the offerings. Very soon after this announcement in church by Monda, he developed what they called the "tithes disease". He developed Parkinsonism, but the public, not knowing of the syndrome, explained that these were the same hands he had been using to pinch the tithes that were now being punished by the Almighty God.

On another occasion just after the elections, Monda was in the market place chastising or, as it were, publicly denouncing some of the politicians. He announced that some of them bribed to get votes. By a stroke of bad luck, one of the contestants happened to be in sight and Monda declared him as one of those who bribed and bribed extensively. Monda announced that people were not foolish. They could see through him and they didn't vote him in. This offended the contestant to the extent that there ensued some confrontation between him and Monda. As fate will have it, he struck Monda and that was the end of the long life of this villager who made life in the village from time to time exciting and interesting. Needless to say, the prospective candidate had to endure many years of going up and down remand cells while investigations continued to find why he killed this harmless individual, as people knew him.

One of the people who missed Monda very much was Mr Orina, who remembered him as that gentleman who once he heard that master Orina had gone onto a boarding school, from time to time would find reason to go and visit him. As he would go through the market place, he would conjure a trick to obtain resources for free! Rolling his eyes up and down, round and round, he would make the women selling vegetables mistake this to be a warning of impending violence. The women would run away and leave their vegetables. He would then arm himself with sufficient amounts of these green, fresh vegetables, and tomatoes, and proceed to where Orina was residing and present the provisions that were highly appreciated and needed at that moment in time. As a student from the village, you are left to your own devices once you went to boarding school. Boarding school often meant you went and built a shack outside the compound of the school or within the compound of the school and fended for yourself. Whenever Monda appeared, everybody knew that a fresh surprise had arrived.

It was also in the same station where Salimo happened to interact and make friends with the engineer who claimed to have danced with the Queen of England. It's the same place where he had to resuscitate him, having been a victim of assault by undisciplined force. This undisciplined force was meted by a few members of the police force who were rogue and did not always abide by the law. For them, interrogation meant anything short of waterboarding. They would start with crashing the testicles, as they believed that testosterone was the root cause of the problems afflicting many of the offenders. Among many of the conditions that Salimo was expected to attend to, were injuries from gunshots. For the district was not too far from Amin-ravaged Uganda. Or arrows in the chest. The arrows were from the injuries sustained during cattle wrestling encounters among the ethnic groups fighting for pasture, or water, or land, or all of them together. Salimo soon became a very highly specialised person in terms of trauma management without any additional training.

One of the incidents that deserves to be mentioned – this was again occasioned by an encounter with Monda; Monda disliked politicians always suspicious about politicians. Monda was the one who declared that politicians in the African continent, many of them, were born of a difficult breech. How he came to know that many of them were born of a difficult breech, no one knew and we will never know. It was clear that in the village a breech delivery was first of all a wrong way out. From experience the outcome was not good, either the baby died or the baby and mother died, or the baby born had some overt symptom or covert brain problems. Therefore Monda had concluded that the most likely explanation of all the aberrations in political operations that one can encounter in the African continent he, Monda, could explain it on the basis that a proportion of these leaders were born of a difficult breech. How else could they continue repeating the same mistakes that those who had gone before them repeated or committed?

Probably by a conspiracy of events, during the same year in a neighbouring constituency a seasoned politician found himself entangled in a legal battle of his life having been charged for allegedly shooting to death a young voter, Uhuru Ndege, for disturbances at a political rally. Although discharged on all counts, in the court of public opinion he remained guilty and in the view of the people Uhuru Ndege was vindicated after the politician suffered a stroke sometimes later.

The village people would shake heads in agreement of their verdict of guilt; justifying it based on the unconfirmed story that while preparing to shoot into outer space, the recently excavated skull of Uhuru Ndege that had been clandestinely delivered to his front door, the politician instead collapsed and henceforth lost the use of his right leg!

It was while in this district that Salimo would have his second encounter with Arap Moi. This face-to-face encounter was most unexpected and most dramatic. Multi-party politics was in the air. The young were fighting for their rights. Moi's government had grown as intolerant as Jomo Kenyatta's was. He had even detained many people, conjuring up all kinds of crimes imagined or actually committed to incarcerate some of the strong opponents of the regime. Indeed it was at this time when many of them also opted to seek asylum elsewhere in other countries. For the first time during Moi's regime, Kenyans had their eyes and minds opened up to the larger world outside, until then everybody was "homed-in" or was inward-looking, believing in what the politician described as Kenya being the island of peace. During this time, cyberspace was still not open to ordinary mortals which normal Kenyans were considered to be.

Indeed from time to time Moi would say, "Look all around us. East, West, North, only the South was peaceful. Look at how many refugees that there are seeking asylum in the country from Somalia, from Sudan, from Ethiopia, from Uganda, you name it." Therefore Moi would conclude by warning particularly the clergy who were often protected by their calling and were the most outspoken during this time. Indeed this generated the famous Moi saying, "Leave politics to politicians." He would admonish the clergy who were engaging in politics. Little did he know that the church and politics are inseparable. Both of them seek to realise the best for society. The church seeks to take them to heaven and to bring equity and equality; the politicians are also saying they're striving to promote the welfare of the fellow human beings! It was very difficult to understand how Moi and his ilk came up with the idea that there was a race born to be politicians and another race born to be clergy, and a majority who were born to depend on the clergy and the politicians for their deliverance from earthly bondage!

Indeed this is the time when one of the outspoken clerics, Arap Muge himself, became extremely vocal against the ills of the government ranging from corruption, to murder, and all manner of evil. So virulent was his attack on government that one local politician warned that he had better not set foot in his constituency or he would never come back alive. Unfortunately for this politician, who was incidentally the same one who at independence had declared that he would not serve in a black man's government; he had acquired so much expensive education that was only good in the service of the queen's government. When Jomo Kenyatta appointed him a permanent secretary he declined with some degree of arrogance! Needless to say with his education he was able to amass immense wealth. However, he had gone a step too far when he declared that should the Bishop set his foot in his constituency, he would not go back alive. Unfortunately Bishop Muge, not wanting to let down his congregation, one Sunday morning drove in the company of a few of them to this place, the very constituency of fate. They had prayers and a good day out, but on his way back the car was involved in a head-on collision with a truck the Bishop died on the spot. He was the only passenger who passed away.

Now the blame game started. The prophecy of doom started, and the poor politician had to resign from his cabinet post. Paradoxically, time and tides wait for no man. When he realised that, first the Queen's government was gone for good, that from then onwards there would only be a government led by black people, and that despite his immense wealth he did not command anybody, he decided to venture into the Hall Of Fame, which according to Moi, was the political arena. This in some way is seen in most of these countries as the ultimate. You could be whatever you are. You could be a professor, you could be whatever you are, eventually when you retire from your profession, you're manning the final post where nobody retires, there's no retirement age in that profession. You become a politician.

The self-confessed black man who only is fit to serve the Queen's government realised that he'd reached that age where he needed to join this career where all those who think they're successful, whether it be from business, from professions, or from administrative post, this is where they retired to. From there on, it's only the Almighty God who decides when to retire you. You continue until you meet your end on earth. Such was the time when Salimo was in this district, and from time to time encountered the negative side of the politics of the nation. At least at this time some sense was the returning into the nation; thanks to those who thought of the strategy of district focus for rural development. It was the slow path back to the original constitution that was signed by the Queen in Chamber that gave Kenya its independence. It created regional governments, and it created councils, and devolved the governing structure. Though it was designed to protect the interests of the various ethnic tribes of the country the inklings of development from the grass roots it took another easily 20 to 25 years, for the nation to go the full cycle back to the constitutional order signed by Her Majesty the Queen in Chamber.

***

The key feature of Moi's long reign was corruption and a transformation from tolerance to intolerance and lastly a transformation of institutions from all established institutions to glamorous, short-lived institutions. Of the glamorous, short-lived institutions, one can identify three of the most important ones: one; the Nyayo Car, two; the London Buses, three; the London Taxis.

But one can also identify these attempts to reform the education system as well as the attempt to reform the electro process. The Nyayo Buses were part of the grand idea to provide inexpensive transport system to the masses. Moi's mind had come to the conclusion that, what was required is government to form the Nyayo Bus Company.

Indeed, the Nyayo Bus Company was established as a state corporation with the powers to manage and run the public transport system, known as the Nyayo Bus Services. This was a grandiose idea that lived for only the briefest of moments.

Wherever the source of funds came from, buses were procured and started operating on most roads of the Republic, but their lifetime was as brief as the time it took to conceive and implement the idea. Many of them lie in different cities and towns as empty shells that reflect a short-lived but active life. Did the government make money out of this? Difficult to tell, but the fact that the Nyayo Bus Company wound up before it was in its adolescence tells the full story.

Then came the realisation that the public taxi system was old-fashioned, run down and an embarrassment, generally, to the Republic, so once more, the great leader conjured up an idea of transforming the city of Nairobi of a replica of the city of London.

With this, the project was hatched to procure look-alike London taxis, new, that would be made available at affordable prices to the many drivers who were running the taxi system, particularly in the city of Nairobi, where the Japanese-made old cars were an eyesore.

Once more, the political elite formed this company that imported these super dudes (as they were called by some doctors) that were exactly of the same look, the same make and the same size. On the streets they were London taxis in the wrong city.

Once more, Moi was effective in promoting these ideas; they were promoted using the best and most effective slogans used in a manner that made it appeal like it was God-sent and that from now on the image of the taxis will change for good.

The London taxis lasted a little longer than Nyayo buses, presumably because they were managed by only a few hands and therefore, it was possible to keep them running a little longer. Surprisingly, one would find these taxis not just in the city of Nairobi, but along all the main roads and main arteries feeding the city of Nairobi.

Needless to say, this scheme, whether it was intended to enrich the poor taxi owners in the city of Nairobi, or the importers, was as equally short-lived as the Nyayo Bus system.

Then came one of the grandest ideas; the leader decided that it was high time that the people drove a car made in the country, for the country, by the country itself, a truly Nyayo project.

Give the devil his due! Arap Moi assembled a team of engineers from all systems, the railroad system, which was famed to have one of the best workshops in East Africa, the

University of Nairobi and other entities that were in productive engineering in the country.

Once more, the Nyayo Car Company was established and given resources to develop the engine block and to develop the body works and the name of Uhuru. In a project shrouded with secrecy, centred around the University of Nairobi and the railway engineering workshop, work went on without break, because apparently there was some deadline that Arap Moi had set for the project to produce results.

Indeed, as the project went on, from time to time the whole government retinue would be paraded in the workshop with cameras rolling and TV and newsprint media moguls accompany the state visitors to the workshop. While there was no conveyor belt and no observable production line, nevertheless it was clear that something momentous was happening; something important would come out of this project.

The project neared completion, and as usual, the public was kept informed about the great Kenyan invention; that soon every Kenyan would have an affordable car that is truly Kenyan. On this important occasion when the car was now said to be almost complete, a ceremony was arranged to launch this brand new model, Uhuru One; made in Kenya, by Kenyans, for Kenyans.

The launching was not to be at the workshop, but at the great stadium bearing the name of Nyayo, the popular name for Arap Moi himself. After a brief address to the gathering, time came for the car to take its maiden drive. At the wheel was Arap Moi himself. He did not want to miss the occasion to launch a truly nationalistic car.

The car started, the car was set, everything was set and Arap Moi then switched on the ignition of the car and set it in motion around the stadium. To the great jubilation of the gathered crowd, the car was actually moving and it went around and to the starting point. Arap Moi brought the car to a smooth stop and to the waving of the crowd who were urging him to take a second round.

He went back to the ignition and tried to start the car. The animal heaved and quivered violently, followed by a violent convulsion ending into total silence. To the great horror and the embarrassment of everybody, the car refused to start despite many desperate efforts to kick it back to life, opening the bonnet by the engineers to check what was wrong – whether it was something minor, but nevertheless, this monumental achievement of the Nyayo era was unable to be resuscitated back into life.

Indeed, before the car was set into motion, there had been a brief ceremony for many investors to pledge their wish to buy shares in this company. Many of the state corporations that specialised in finance; endowment funds, pension funds, medical insurance, all pledged to purchase significant proportions of shares in this Nyayo project. It was, therefore, a great letdown when the Nyayo car died only after 500 meters of action.

There ended yet another epic Nyayo project born in a great drama, yet unable to deliver. The great leader was a man of vision and a man of ideas, no wonder he had been nicknamed, "The Giraffe" by no other than the great Oginga Odinga who had watched this great son from Rift Valley grow from a high school teacher into a member of the legislative assembly, before eventually rising to the office of the vice-president of the Republic.

No one could have imagined that a man from such a region could start so low yet go so high. Indeed, his rule, his reign remains and probably will remain the only one that spanned two decades. Looking back at his old days and probably using his old experience of things he didn't like about the education system, he conjured an idea of a reform.

First of all, he came with the new mathematics. Which used base one instead of base 10. Arap Moi had decided that Kenya needed to come to the computer age and the computer age only worked on the scale of one or zero. Kenyan children needed to be brought to the new era. Unfortunately, when they started adding and saying one plus one is 20, the public would not understand the logic.

Soon, there were all manner of complaints and criticism of this new system. Nobody understood what problem it was intended to solve and how that would make the life of Kenyans better. Hearing a backlash, the government retracted and said, "No, there was no need to go that route." A commission was set into motion to study how best to do it.

The great leader eventually came up with what he considered the greatest transformation of the educational system in Kenya, to do away with the advanced level and set up what he called, "Eight-four-four".

This meant eight primary, four secondary and four university years. This was intended, among other things, to bring equity into the educational system considering the number of communities that had no access to the advanced level, or schools that provided advanced level education.

Therefore, taking everybody from 12 years of education and putting them in university, gave everybody in the country a level playing ground. To its credit, this system did stick and indeed realise the fruits that it was intended to realise, which was the massive expansion of the educational system in the country.

Indeed, with this project, one can say that Arap Moi had an enduring impact on the educational system and possibly, the future of the Republic, given that education plays a great role in national development. The other great innovation of the Nyayo government, or Arap Moi's regime, was taking corruption to the greatest heights in the nation.

It would take a long time for this record to be broken, it was unparalleled. Anything that could be stolen, was stolen, anything that could be used to pilfer government resources was put in motion. It's like the appointees of the state would from time to time meet and hold a competition of who has amassed the greatest wealth or has come with the grandest scheme to skim off the cream of the national economy.

No sector was left untouched. Whether it be the road, the industry, you name it; all sectors were affected. Unfortunately, whenever there is corruption, there are some sectors where the impact shows immediately. One of them is the health sector. During this regime, corruption was most virulent in the health sector probably to be eclipsed by the imaginary gold export scandal in Kenya, the so-called Goldenberg scandal!

The two combined immediately started to show the negative sides of an uncontrolled corruption. Shortage of drugs, equipment which was not functioning, no ambulances, disgruntled health workers and a sharp upward spike in infant mortality. It's unclear how the nation reached this level of corruption. Some people considered it as an overreaction or knee-jerk reaction to the attempted coup.

During the coup, for the first time, those in power realised how temporary their tenure is and that their principal employer, the public can be an ass. Therefore it's like a decision was taken for those in power to perfect their skills in crafting corrupt practices that benefited the few.

For Salimo this provided a fertile ground for materials for the *Medicus* newsletter. Repeated articles were printed in the newsletter vividly describing the magnitude of the cancer that was eating at every sector of the economy. These articles did not go unnoticed. Indeed, the pioneers of the multi-party political movement realised that this information could be important in getting their message of change heard.

One of the plans they decided on was to bring the evil face-to-face with the boss himself. For evidence, they decided to enlist the services of the editors of medicals. This is where Salimo found himself once more face-to-face with Arap Moi.

After many failed efforts to reach Arap Moi, one day, Salimo was summoned by his fellow activists in the fight against the vice. He was required to be in a city early afternoon for the appointment where Arap Moi was at four o'clock tea.

At that stage, there was no flight from the far away district where Salimo was working, so he set off in the early hours of the morning in the old Land Rover GK100X that was tired, overused and required form time to time to be stopped for it to cool down before they could proceed.

Indeed, Salimo was not aware that plans for this meeting were so advanced that he was expected to reach at two o'clock and by four o'clock be seated next to the great leader. Therefore, by the time he arrived in the city, it was four o'clock, obviously too late for the English teatime.

A rearrangement of the program was quickly agreed with the great leader and it was agreed that this now would be transformed from a four o'clock tea break into a full-grown breakfast meeting with the president. This was the first time that Salimo realised how serious his compatriots were in exposing the rise of corruption to His Excellency himself.

***

Maybe the greatest achievement in Moi's government as he kept tinkering with education was the foresight to imagine and bring into being the second medical school in the country. Until then, the Royal Technical College that was inherited from the colonial government and transformed into the University of Nairobi was the premier institution of higher learning. It embodied the brilliant spirit of the nation and had its Chancellor, initially, Jomo Kenyatta himself before handing over the mantle to Arap Moi.

Unfortunately the university did not always live to the expected reputation, given the many incidences of confrontation with the law. Ultimately the diagnosis was made that the university was not a reflection of the true spirit of the ordinary Kenyan and farther the diagnosis went on, the key problem was its location in the centre of the city, next to the ill-fated Uhuru Highway! Indeed, it was a commonly held opinion that the students did not have a mechanism of making their grievances known, particularly through the confrontation with the other law-abiding citizens, who were running around their businesses only to encounter stone-throwing mobs from the university.

So great was the nuisance of these mobs, as they were described, that it was determined that to solve this problem once and for all, there should be no farther expansion of this institution within the city perimeters and that in future whenever there was opportunity to start another university, it would be best placed in the rural areas or in such a place that should the same demon that had invaded this university also emerge in that institution, then the means of expressing this disagreement was greatly reduced, so it was argued. The students would have to contend with docile villagers, farmers or farm animals, depending on where it would be eventually located.

Through a thoroughly researched process, headed by some pioneer educationist, it was resolved but not unexpected that the institution should be located within the heart of the Rift Valley, far away from any settled urban centre. As usually happens, these kinds of engagements and endeavours can have a profound impact on the lives of many others who otherwise would have led a different life.

So for Salimo, the possibility of a second university brought with it the romance of the rural areas. He did not intend to go there, but ended up there through a roundabout way. The famous professional association, intending to expand and grow its wings, imagined big dreams of increasing the capacity of doctors and health workers who found themselves in hard to reach areas; not only hard to reach for the patients or for themselves and their families, but also for new knowledge.

The Association therefore thought that it was its ethical responsibility to provide their colleagues who were in isolated places a means of furthering their knowledge and a way of supporting them through educational materials and information. Salimo was nominated as a potential educator, to be trained on how to develop and manage educational programs through a distance learning processes. At this stage, the only models which were available were from the West Indies where multiple campuses in different islands were connected through crude methods or mechanisms like packet radio through which educational information could be exchanged and professionals in isolated communities could be linked and made to feel that they were part of a network of healthcare providers.

Through a combination of events best described as coincidence or conspiracy of events, Salimo found himself consigned to go and be part of the pioneer faculty for the new university's School of Medicine. His mentor, the dean of the medical school, having identified him and having noted that he had a particular affinity for the city where the medical school or possibly a teaching hospital would be located, dispatched him to this institution with instructions to transform the existing district rural hospital, into a teaching and referral facility.

Characteristic to Salimo, he inserted in this project his heart, mind, and soul, enabling the institution to take off with a wave of some elements of modern educational methods and also with a promise that the product that would come out of this school would be of the kind that would deliver most health communities of the scourge that is ill-health and disease. The school would adopt a recently introduced methodology of training known as problem-based learning. At this stage, only a few renowned medical schools in Australia, Europe and Canada had espoused this new approach of training doctors.

In its simplest form, it can be described as overturning, and overthrowing the pyramid of education, a pyramid that until then held that to train a health professional he had to be prepared with their foundational knowledge of science that would form the basis for the clinical year that followed. Over the years, it had been noted that whereas science is the foundation in view of the explosion of new knowledge and scientific part, in medicine particularly, it was not possible for any ordinary doctor to amass the body of knowledge that was required or was necessary to practise medicine at the contemporary time and in future. In any event, it was clear that probably the amount of difficult information, had stripped the capacity of the human mind to store facts and to reproduce them at the opportune moment, so new education, particularly from McMaster developed a new way of enabling the student to organise knowledge so that at the opportune moment they can re-use it.

The new paradigm shift was that instead of starting with the normal mechanisms and normal scientific processes, once you started from the abnormal and knew the abnormal, it would generate interest in learning and dissecting and analysing knowledge, starting from the problem; thus a student would move away from simply imbibing facts and applying facts and organising, and would start solving future health problems.

In a nut shell, the starting point of learning would be an abnormal stage or an abnormal state of the human body, prompting the young mind to be curious to discover why it became abnormal and what changes would explain the abnormality – these changes are embedded in the basic sciences. In other words, the learning of basic sciences and clinical sciences would be integrated into one holistic core, enabling the student to have the hooks upon which to hang the new knowledge, and apply it as required.

For the most traditional clinicians, this was too radical and too sweet to be true. So while there was a strong movement to transform medical education in line with this new thought, in the same vein this generated reaction forces amongst the traditionalists who thought these would undermine their capacity to control learning or to ensure that a student learned the same way they learned themselves. However, since this was a brand new medical school and the movement for change was extremely strong and there were also resources available worldwide, coupled with the "Health for All" declaration of Alma Ata, which brought to the fore the issues of community health and the continual care from the household to the most advanced hospital, a combination of a community-oriented education and problems, this learning strategy offered the most important tool for educating the health professionals of the future.

It was not difficult to convince many donors and national agencies to invest time and resources into the new medical school that Kenya was establishing. Fortunately for Salimo, he had the good luck to be mentored by one of those proponents of the system and a medical educationist who pioneered this process in Newcastle, Australia. Charles Engels was his mentor for one year and it didn't take long for Salimo to realise all that was wrong with the way he was taught in medical school and the possibility that something could be changed. He needed no convincing because the arguments spoke for themselves. Indeed, by the time he joined this medical school, he had outlined what he considered the undergraduate program objectives for the new medical school and he said that was how to convince colleagues from the old school of thought that this was the way to go.

Most new to controversy and change into transformation, Salimo therefore arrived in this new station with the conviction that this was God sent, that what he had learned in theory, he put it in practice and not in a micro but in a macro scale. This action by Arap Moi to create a new second medical school marked the second turning point in Salimo's life as he moved on from being purely a clinician to becoming an educationist. And from there on, his new life was cut for him.

Arriving at the new station, he found his new boss in the office answering a long distance call, at the end of which he informed the other person on the other end that it was up to the Vice Chancellor to work with him in his way or keep his job. And so, Salimo was introduced into his new job in the midst of this controversy where the Vice Chancellor was making some demands and the newly appointed dean was turning around and let it be known by all and sundry that he would not be pushed around. His mentor, Professor Thomas Ogada, did not throw him in the deep end without a life jacket. Indeed, he also followed it with some leads on where he could find resources and how he might go about creating this new institution together with how to bring together a team.

From the first day he arrived; looking at the district hospital, it was clear to Salimo that this was not a walk in the park. It was, indeed, a university school and medical school, it was postgraduate, it wasn't just the routines of opening abdomens and closing abdomens, a system that had been set years past that one only needed to master the art. The government did not provide any meaningful resources for this new project besides giving the dean a one-roomed office, a secretary, a desk and four chairs. The dean was challenged to come up with a strategy for ensuring that the teaching hospital would be developed.

The new dean and his protégé, or his handyman as he was described, soon found their rhythm and brought together a team of diverse medical specialties, often from the existing university. Pushing them, for the first time, to develop a truly written curriculum of a medical school was no easy task. Indeed, from time to time, it was clear that the project may never take off. Not only because there were limited resources and limited government funding, but also because of their ideology. The ideology was foreign and known to be subject to misinterpretation.

Indeed, the mere notion that in the problem-based learning situation, the lecturer is not the centre of knowledge to the student, the mere notion that there will be minimal lectures or none and the students will use problems and generate knowledge and learning through discourse with the lecturer, or the lecturer profession acting as the referee, was the antithesis of creating a health professional. Also, in great detail, the old school of thought expounded their disdain and opposing viewpoints.

From time to time, the couple found themselves having to build their defence, pushing against thick walls, often confronted with emotionally charged non-academic or pseudo-political criticisms. Many prophets of doom declared with conviction "What will come out of this medical school will be Chinese barefoot doctors". On one such occasion, the duo was summoned to the senate and directed to go and destroy all they what had written, and use the curriculum from the established medical school at the University of Nairobi.

At this stage, the two had been lambasted from left, right and centre to the point of submission and acquiescence, so to say. They humbly requested the Vice Chancellor to provide them with the text of the curriculum from the mother medical school. Fortunately for them, in the old medical school, the curriculum was described very briefly in the context of year one: 100 hours of anatomy, 200 hours of physiology or 300 hours of this and that. What was taught in these 100 hours, or 200 hours, or 300 hours was not explicit. Hence, when this document was placed before the university council and then vice senate and even to the grand master, Arap Moi himself, looking at both documents, he immediately saw the wisdom of having a more comprehensive document as was being proposed in the second medical school.

Making a U-turn, he directed that the mother medical school ought to learn from the daughter medical school. And with that in mind, the couple were encouraged to move full speed ahead and given two years within which to have an intake of 40 medical students. Having no resources from the state and no budget from the university, the first activity of the curriculum after it was written, was to market it amongst the key financial institutions and to find suitable partners in Sweden and in Netherlands who were inclined to support an institution which promised change and transformation of learning and a new cadre of health professionals.

Therefore, it was not surprising that some of the earliest funding came from such old institutions like the Swedish development agency or agencies from Netherlands. Indeed, within the space of three years, the duo had been able to attract a few more enthusiastic and unconventional clinicians to join them. They had identified partner institutions in Sweden and in the USA and in the UK. With these partners, and funding from the Swedish government, they were able to create a semblance of physical facilities that would accommodate 40 students, would provide teaching and learning facilities, and provide them with a base to continue to grow.

Through this conspiracy of events, Salimo was fortunate enough to have interacted with stalwarts of educational development and transformation such as the great Edward Perry and Charles Engels, among many others. People who had devoted all their lives trying to change something, trying to improve something, trying to do things differently and if having reached crossroads they chose the less-beaten path, much to their surprise of what extent they succeeded to.

The project might have died yet at the infancy after the university management was not fully convinced about the experimental approach to medical education, so they commissioned a one-man study to determine whether this project was valuable. For the assignment, they identified a prominent legal mind who was not only renowned in politics, but a key figure in making the historic Kenya Airways a success story.

Arriving at the institution with profound ideas, it was not difficult for him to poke holes into the whole project. Indeed, in his conclusion and his submission to the senate, this one-man commission, Isaac, pronounced himself very clearly when he said, "Gentleman, if I were you, I'll go and tell the Kenya government that this is an impossible task. It cannot be done. And I'd advise the government to close down the government school before it is even started."

Undeterred, Salimo felt obliged to respond immediately and his simple answer was, "Sir, whereas legal logic would say this cannot be done, it is my submission, sir, that this medical school is going to start, it's going to grow, and it will be an institution of great repute and a centre of excellence."

Then Isaac retorted, "Well, good luck." And with that, he left the senate meeting.

As fate would have it, almost 30 years later in downtown Windhoek, the two would cross paths again as the great Isaac accompanied a delegation of yet another Kenyatta who was attending the inaugural ceremony of a new president. When he was introduced to this younger gentleman, he immediately remembered and said, "Oh, many years ago I went to Eldoret to the centre of the new medical school and had some tiff with some young man there." And the young man, now an older man, announced that yes, indeed, he was the younger man.

Isaac, thereafter, immediately was full of praise. He said, "Every now and again I go to that medical school and I remember the encounter and the conviction with which you announced that it would be a great institution. Congratulations."

Isaac shortly followed this with an equally elevating email which read in part:

"Dear Prof, it was a pleasure to meet you after our first meeting in Eldoret so any years ago. Although we did not meet

again after our long wait to see President Uhuru, what you have done for our Namibian friends made me happy and proud of you and your achievement. As a teacher, you have already touched the lives of many people. Work in the health field is a calling."

It was at his engagement with the first new medical school that Salimo met and befriended one of his thereafter close, or almost fraternal, friends, Engineer Kimani. The two of them heated together. Both of them had their families in the city of Nairobi. Both of them commuted regularly from Nairobi to the city and back. Indeed, Salimo claimed that in one year, he did easily 20 thousand kilometres commuting between Nairobi and the new medical school. The two were involved in the site meetings and discussions of the new structure and in looking for associates.

At this stage, with the admission of the new group of students, the project started attracting resources and the vast main injection was from leftover funds used to construct the national stadium. At that stage, the Chinese were at the craze of building stadia in the African continent. So, they invested substantial amounts of money in the construction of the only national stadium at that stage. A combination of working fast and using cheap labour saved them a sizeable amount of money that could translate to four million US dollars at that time's exchange rate. This was a huge sum by any imagination.

Tipped by an insider, the dean and his protégé then produced a proposal and a submission to Arap Moi himself, indicating that they were a worthwhile project and that there would be a high return on investment if the money was given to the medical school instead of building a glass factory somewhere in the area the neighbourhoods of the infamous Manyani. Not surprisingly, the government obliged and gave the entire amount to the new project enabling the university, for the first time, to construct physical facilities, accommodation, and staff accommodation as well as lecture theatres for the new medical school.

Gradually, the medical school started to take shape, started to attract new lecturers and professors, new partners, and new ideas and research. Indeed, the project was marketed as the second teaching and referral hospital in the country, taking care of the western cluster of the national population.

The new school may have sounded grandiose, but at the end of the day, this project realised its dream. Indeed, when AIDS was a fully blown epidemic in the country, this project was the first one to undertake community-based testing, community-based counselling as well as community-based and home-based care for the patient who was affected by HIV and AIDS. So successful was the project that all the great ones, including Bill Gates, were convinced that there was a worthwhile project to invest their resources in. It's not surprising therefore that from time to time Bill Gates would be seen walking through the streets of the rural town like any ordinary Kenyan citizen and not the rich and the mighty of the West.

It was while working on this project that the paths of Haroun, Naimara, Salimo and Kimani crossed and crisscrossed thereafter. It is while developing this project that the Kaptula lady came into the picture. It was while working on this project that Engineer Kimani and Salimo went on to do even greater things. Engineer Kimani went on to become eventually a cabinet secretary while Salimo continued with his endeavour of founding new medical schools in the continent.

It was while working in this project that Salimo's notion of motions and *Hakuna Matata* also took root. For example, it was not uncommon for them to hitchhike a lift to the city Nairobi and hitchhike a lift back to the new medical school. Or hitchhike a lift to the village or drive to the village with a minimum of resources. On such an occasion, Engineer Kimani invited Salimo to accompany him to a funeral and between themselves, they had just enough cash to fill the guzzler in the SUV and drive it to the village and back. They had no reserve. But Engineer Kimani, himself great believer of Hakuna Matata, had no difficulty in convincing Salimo that all would be well, so off they went. Little did they know that when you go to a village for a funeral, you must expect the unexpected.

And so, at the funeral, the grandmother of Salimo insisted that she must be dropped several kilometres away from the destined location and others also had to be dropped here and there. The short story is that on the way back the SUV developed a problem and it required repairs before they could proceed. The brakes jammed. The first problem to solve was to find the mechanic at 6 PM on a Saturday in a city where the majority of the people were Seventh Day Adventists. A few telephone calls, for Salimo knew his way around the town, enabled them to find a mechanic who knew an Indian merchant who was willing to come and open the shop at 6 o'clock on Saturday evening so that they could get a new set of drums for the brakes and the other spare parts. And with these repairs, all the money for petrol was spent. And still, Engineer Kimani insisted, "Don't worry," Daktari as he called him. "Don't worry. We'll find our way. You know the secretary of the Lions Club; we will find a lion here, it will be sorted out," he announced.

Indeed, soon they were able to find the secretary or the treasurer for the movement in that town. He was a successful businessman; when they found him, he was actually taking stock of the day's business and accounting for the day's earning. Once the problem was explained to him, he was swift to inform them that he actually had no cash of his own. Everything else he was holding was company money and therefore, he politely declined any support.

Quick thinking, Engineer Kimani announced that the best way is to do whatever any logical person would do, and that is to carry some passengers and generate the gasoline money as they drove the way back. With Salimo as the tout or as the *manamba* as he is called in the city, hassling passengers into the SUV was indeed not difficult because at this late hour usually there were many desperate travellers. So, soon they had three or four passengers and by their calculation that was enough to take them halfway. They believed that having reached halfway they could find another three or four passengers to take them the full length of the journey.

While they were busy finding the fourth passenger, Engineer Kimani from a distance saw one of his relatives and announced that the problems for the evening had been sorted out and that there was no point in loading the SUV with passengers anymore. And with that, they announced that the trip had been terminated, they were not going any further. So, driving to the sister-in-law of Engineer Kimani, whom he already described as his saviour, he proceeded to explain the predicament. To their surprise, the sister had known not only that the tank should be filled to the brim, she continued to give them additional resources for fuelling on the way and even before letting them go, invited them for a warm dinner of boiled bananas. And from there on, Engineer Kimani could not stop telling the doctor how this particular sister-in-law had saved him from the trying moments and circumstances. The rest of the trip was uneventful and they arrived safely at midnight.

As soon as they touched down in the local city, Engineer Kimani came up with the idea of going and cooling it out. And so, they left one local partner to go to the nightspot. Halfway through cooling it off, as it was described, it was difficult to imagine that the same people who were destitute; unable to finance their trip back, were now in the company of glittering ladies in glittering attire, only from time to time waltzing in the grass even before reaching the dance hall. That was the friendship that the two of them vouched for a long time to come and that eventually, once more, found them in the midst of the conversation with Isaac downtown Windhoek, with Engineer Kimani now the cabinet minister, and Salimo as dean of the medical school.

For Salimo and Engineer Kimani, the construction project went on very fast but it also illustrated the tension between a Chinese construction company which had financed some part of the project, in that the finances were coming from China, doing the construction work in Africa. From time to time, there would be occasions when Engineer Kimani would come and condemn some aspect of the project. And on one occasion this delayed the project for about six months for the simple reason that the contractor had conspired to use bricks for the walls instead of the stipulated natural grey stone. When Engineer Kimani protested and ordered the walls to be brought down, the contractor then invoked the law that changes were to be authorised from the ministry of the development corporation right back in Peking and for credence, needed to be described in detail, first in English then translated into Chinese and transmitted back home.

When the grievance reached Peking, the information coming back indicated that the honourable minister was somewhere in the provinces and trying to spur development in rural China and would only be back in the city during the great assembly meeting. And therefore, nothing would go on until he came back, to authorise that additional resources could be expended to replace the loss of materials as a result of using wrong stones.

Indeed, the project also brought to notice the characteristic differences between approaches to development by the Chinese and the cultural differences, so to say. The Chinese construction workers were literally confined in their ghetto and were only allowed out very rarely and periodically. It also didn't require a big team to make a monumental impact. Indeed, the construction was going on in the third floor, without any need for cranes or high calibre equipment other than human beings. Indeed, the project once more was completed in record time and with some degree of finesse. For Salimo, this was yet an occasion to solidify the belief in life: why worry, usually there were some ideas on how things could work, so why worry? One needed to just walk around and look around; generally solutions could be found.

***

With Engineer Kimani one had to expect the unexpected. And soon enough, it would happen. Engineer Kimani one of these days decided that it would be an economic measure, that Salimo and him this time, don't take their cars to travel to the teaching hostel from the city but instead there will be a form of relay transport to the teaching facility. The first half of the journey would be with a colleague whom Albert Gallachi had nicknamed the piglet.

The piglet would deliver them halfway by two o'clock. Here, they would wait for Charles, the finance man as they call him, to arrive at this midway station where he would be spending the weekend. Then, Engineer Kimani and Salimo would take the transport that would drop Charles back to the teaching hostel. Before they left, Engineer Kimani decided to call the resident engineer on site and inform him of these arrangements.

He called the voice on the other side of the line, on hearing that it was Engineer Kimani, responded rather too promptly, "No, Engineer Kimani no here," and banged down the receiver. Then Engineer Kimani again called. The Chinese voice on the other side again came on the line, saying, "Engineer Kimani, Engineer Kimani, no here. Engineer Kimani ee, Engineer Kimani go see wifer," and banged down the phone.

In order to get this message, the engineer decided to use a different approach. This time he dialled and said, "This is

Engineer Kimani, it is Engineer Kimani here, can I talk to Chou?"

"Chou? Aha! Chou, wait." So then Engineer Kimani was able to relay the message. This was generally the mode of communication with the Chinese team on the ground.

Having informed his counterpart in the station, the piglet arrived promptly on time, and the trip to the halfway station went on uneventfully. However, it was quite clear that Charles was having a problem setting off and thereafter arriving at the halfway station. In the absence of mobile phones, the engineer and Salimo opted to use the traditional telephone box by the post office. Unfortunately, a storm also was on the way, and as soon as they entered the red box, it started to pour what would be described as cats and dogs.

So intense was the rainfall that soon the telephone booth was flooded, and very quickly the water was already above their cuffs. Needless to say, their shoes were full of water. Abandoning the intention to call, the pair made a dash for the shelter at the nearby market station. In this part of the world, when it rains, it pours. Indeed, by the time the pair were under the roof, there was probably no need for them to take shelter anymore. They might as well have stayed in the rain for they were soaked down to their chest.

They continued to expect the arrival of Charles, which did not materialise. Resorting to the only option available to them, the pair then decided that the best way was to go by bus. Once on the bus, which was also full to the brim, the pair did not even have a place to sit, and they thought it wise to sit next to the driver, just above the engine. They figured out that this place would be hot enough to warm them for the rest of the trip.

Indeed, it was nice and comfortable, but the coats and the clothing, having been so thoroughly soaked, were now steaming and very soon the driver was complaining about his inability to navigate, as the steam was covering the windscreen from inside. To alleviate the problem, the pair, not wishing to move away from the comforting zone of the heat from the engine, took turns to wipe the windscreen so the driver could see where they were going.

The ordeal lasted easily three hours before the two could emerge out of the bus and wish the rest of the passengers a safe onward trip. One of the passengers was unnecessarily tickled and thought he should say something to the pair. He said, "Gentlemen, we are sorry that you were soaked in the rain. But if you look, what you are leaving behind is like the mist after a heavy downpour. Well wishes and please, look for warm shelter." And with that, the pair emerged from the bus and took a cab to their respective residences; but this not before Engineer Kimani had condemned their lack of thoughtfulness. Indeed, between them, they had four cars, one SUV, a Nissan Saloon, a Mercedes 200 and a Peugeot station wagon.

According to Engineer Kimani, it was therefore not understandable why they chose to subject themselves to this cruel atmospheric insult, given that each of these four vehicles was entirely capable to be their preferred mode of transport. It was therefore resolved that from then on, they will keep one at least one of the cars at either end of their to and fro trip from the city where they went to visit their families and their duty station.

The trip back to the city was better arranged this time. They decided to take one of the minibuses that plied between the city and the teaching hospital on a regular basis. They decided, to save on time, that they would pay for all the empty seats so that they could travel in comfort back to the city. "Doc, this is what we should have done in the first instance on our way down!" Engineer Kimani was lamenting and amused at the same time.

"Yes, one has to learn and learning never ends," responded Salimo.

One of the most exciting parts of this trip back to the city was that one never got bored. The graffiti or the messages printed on the ends of these *matatus* as they were known, was enough to think about, to laugh about and to learn from. For example, these minibuses or *matatus* carried the current affairs, sizzling news of the day, or the month, or the year.

During this time, a number of them were keeping abreast with events in the USA, particularly the impeachment of Bill Clinton. Not one, not two, but many of these mini buses had lurid pictures of Monica Lewinsky, but of course all of them differed in Monica Lewinskys. There were white Monica Lewinskys, there was black Monica Lewinskys, and there were Chinese Monica Lewinskys. In short, there were all types and kinds of Monica Lewinskys, according to the national journalists' best exposition of what Monica Lewinsky would look like to the passengers.

One, which was intriguing, said, "We either take you to the city or to heaven," a morbid reference to the dangers and risks associated with traveling in these *matatus*. Another one read, "Never surrender." From time to time, you would encounter, at low speed, one of these minibuses with music at 1000 decibels. Literally, the *matatus* would be vibrating. And on the return, the moving disco. From time to time, they would encounter an ever-increasing number of roadblocks. These had been nicknamed "the unofficial toll stations". Because at every point, the tout would run out of the *matatus* even before it was stopped, to meet the officers manning the station, and whisper to them in privacy. Then they would walk behind some thicket or let the *matatu* proceed a little bit before they shook hands and the tout would speedily run out to the *matatu* and jump in while it was in motion.

It was impossible to imagine why or how these touts managed to escape being crushed to death, having missed a step or failed to take hold of the handle at the door. It is clear that they were well trained and physically fit. It would be a rare event if one travelled 300 kilometres on this stretch without experiencing a nasty accident. Indeed, as soon as this particular highway was opened, it was nicknamed "the highway to hell". It was smooth, it was straight. During the days before speed governors were introduced, the drivers behaved as if they were perpetually in a Formula One racing contest.

It's unclear why they would be in such a hurry, particularly if they were only going one way. However, with improvements on the road, some of them even tried going to the city and returning the same day, and on some odd occasions, depending on where they were in the queue, they would even make a third trip back to the city. It was while travelling in this minibus that Salimo conjured the idea of owning one for himself. He took measures now to start addressing poverty, which was one of those declared enemies of the nation. He arranged to import one of these second-hand, because these *matatus* were generally second-hand. They are never new.

Salimo found that there was a syndicate which imported these *matatus*, and all you did was simply deposit your money and wait for the Nissan *matatus* to arrive. Usually it will be a closed van with no windows. Probably they were being used as a transporter for transporting luggage or merchandise previously, and now needed to be converted into transporting human merchandise. The first thing that was required was to go to the local Jua Kali garage. This was the under the sun garages which one would find anywhere. They would cut off the metal and fit in windows. They would remove whatever was in the van and fit in chairs. The number of chairs was generally a matter that the *matatus* owners themselves had agreed on. It wasn't a standardised public transport van. No wonder the outcome of an accident involving any of these matatus was grim, given that they never conformed to any standard of public or passenger vehicle requirements.

They were produced in Japan for goods transport, but were used in Kenya for public transport. At this stage, the Japanese may never recognise the same vehicle that a few months ago was shipped from Yokohama or any of those three popular sources of these second-hand *matatus*.

Unfortunately for Salimo, not being very proficient in the business and not understanding that there were many risks involved in this business, he plunged into this high-risk business headlong. Only after the third month did he realise that the risk was higher than suspected before. The returns started to go down exponentially. It was also clear to him that these *matatus*, other than providing a quick transport for the poor and the ones who could not afford their own car, were a source of livelihood, not for the owner. The owner had to share with many others. This included the driver, the tout who also was described as the battery, because whenever the *matatus* was stuck and needed a push, the tout would run out and give it a push. Hence, the name, the battery.

It also provided a regular income for those who manned the official and unofficial traffic control roadblocks. Indeed, in the returns from the driver, there was always a component written to the government of Kenya. It was a fixed amount. There was even another component for another group which was the one at the both ends that would usher in passengers. Ushering in passengers was a tricky business. If you wanted to go quickly, then there were phony passengers to make it look like the *matatus* is almost full. When the true passenger entered on one side, the phony passenger skipped out, and for two, three hours, therefore there was always a call for only one passenger left, and only one passenger left. But in the end, one would not be surprised that out of 17 passengers in the vehicle, the only true passengers were three or four in number. The rest were used as hooks or as bait to tempt the unsuspecting passengers.

Even more importantly, Salimo did not realise that the routes, though licensed by the road transport authority, were heavily controlled by cartels. The cartels consisted of either the owners of matatus on a particular route who wanted to limit the number of new entrants, who demanded an entrance fee for the route. This was not cheap, but a substantial sum. Then, there was another cartel of the Mongikis. These were the underworld guys who controlled the *matatus* business in the city of Nairobi and progressively invaded other cities. They were rough, tough, and menacing. To succeed, one had to also pay for their services. All in all, one could conclude that the business of *matatu* generated a lot of revenue on a daily basis. But, for the owners of the *matatus*, the benefit was probably 50% of the true value of the enterprise.

In the end, it was clear that to succeed, one had to coexist with the ecosystem around the *matatu* business… Needless to say, a lot of these *matatus* were owned by senior police officers and government officials. No wonder they continued to be a menace on the road, until Engineer Kimani tried to bring sense by introducing speed governors. So unpopular were the speed governors that the owners of these vehicles always found another way. They realised that the police officers on the road had no way of determining whether there was a really true speed governor in the car.

The test they gave the *matatus* was for the officer to jump into the *matatu* and take the steering wheel, and push the accelerator to the limit. While it was clear that the *matatu* was going well above the limit of 80 kilometres per hour or 100 kilometres per hour, with the officer driving on the wheel, it was clear that you could probably be doing 150 or 140. The speedometer never went beyond the legal limit. Unknown to the officer, the speedometer indicator was wired. Wired meant that the dial was tampered with so that the speedometer indicator didn't go beyond a certain level. It was mechanically wired not to exceed the speed limit. Therefore, whereas in theory there was a speed governor in the *matatus*, in practice, it was a contraption to deceive the law.

Salimo did not survive long in this enterprise because the second *matatu* that he imported was stolen the day it was supposed to get all the papers to go to the road. Unknown to Salimo, one had to be careful where you fitted the windows, where you fitted the chairs, because there they would make duplicate keys. The car was driven away without any break-in and any struggle. It would appear that on that day, the driver was followed to where he parked and in the middle of the night, the crooks went in and drove away the car, never to be found again. It could not even be found with the famous squadron that had been formed to combat motor vehicle thefts from the city.

With this experience, Salimo concluded that it would be better to limit his expertise to where he was trained: in the practice of medicine and saving lives. In any event, it was clear to him that there was potential conflict of interest in owning any of these *matatus*, which on a regular basis endangered the lives of the people, or led to so much pain and suffering, or if one wanted to look at it in a morbid way, generated work for him. It would be like a doctor owning a business that was making coffins or was a funeral home. The patient's relatives would, should their relative pass away, always have lingering doubts about whether this doctor was letting these patients intentionally move on or check out, as it was popularly known.

***

Having received his dollars as he called it, Antony McOnyango, whose nickname was McAntony, spat on them and waved them in the air and thanked God in the traditional ritual of giving blessing and praise. "Now we can go and enjoy ourselves," he announced as he left the banking hall in a huff. It was difficult to imagine what would befall McAntony later in the day now that he had received his wages, as he called it. The chief executive officer of the institution was flabbergasted when he received a late night telephone call requesting for him to send help for McAntony, who had been retrieved from a drainage ditch in the city. As if that was not enough, McAntony was being extremely provocative to the police and to the politicians.

On the one side, the moment he came out of the ditch, his immediate question to the rescuers was, "Where is my friend Thomas?" He could vaguely remember that the last time he had contact with Tom, they were being confronted by the police and because Tom was less intoxicated he was leading the confrontation and making the police angrier. McAntony could remember that Tom was arrested and was driven into the cells. He could remember that he then for some moment was standing on the other side of the road, for the police station was right in the middle of the town and on the main highway and he was calling at the top of his voice. He was calling, "Serikal, where is Tom? Serikal, where is Tom?" Literally meaning, "You government, where is my colleague, Tom?" If he was in the US, he would be saying, "Uncle Sam, where is Tom?"

On and on he went, until the same cops came for him, but knowing him and looking at him they opted to take a soft line with him and asked him to proceed home if he didn't want trouble. From there on he continued to denounce Arap Moi and his government. He went on to talk about corruption. He went on to broadcast in the middle of the night to whoever could hear or was listening that he is a son of the soil, born of the lake, he was going to do the unthinkable. He was going to ensure that he brought the secretary general of the party to his knees and that in the next general election he was going to emerge victorious.

He continued taunting the police and Moi and the whole government machinery who had exploited the poor, who were enriching themselves and he promised a beating in the next general election for each and every one of them. As he went farther and farther, it looked like he was getting more and more intoxicated. It wasn't clear why this could be so but looking back, it was understandable. Normally there was a closing time when beers could not be served but what the people would do when this eleven o'clock was approaching, i.e. when the bars stopped the supply, they would overstock. They would order more than they could consume in the remaining minutes.

They would then, when the doors had been closed, continue enjoying their beers after hours, as the police used to refer to it, whenever they arrested any of these kinds of people breaking the law. They would be taken to court and be charged for drinking after hours until some smart lawyers came back, dealt a dead blow to these after-hours concepts when one of them asked the court to define for him what the definition of after-hours was and whether there was anything in the books that described these after hours. To the surprise of everybody, all the arrested were set free and from there on the precise time was described whenever someone was charged with drinking after hours.

It is not known what transpired but all that is known is that some equally drunk guys, walking down the road, could hear someone moaning from a drain and on a closer look they realised that it was the great professor who was in trouble. They summoned the ambulance and help from the university. It was this reason why the chief executive was being asked to receive his men. Obviously the chief executive could not drive there himself, so he called someone down the ladder and on and on until a driver was dispatched to the scene to retrieve the great professor.

When information was relayed to the institution about what he had been saying and what had transpired during the day, the CEO concluded that the institution's name had gone down the ditch together with this professor and needed to be redeemed. In particular his pronouncements against the state could be misinterpreted as being held by everybody in the institution and those were not the times when the institution could risk such a slur on the government or would risk being labelled anti-Nyayo.

When McAntony arrived at the hospital casualty, he was a different man. Even Salimo could not recognise him but it was clear that at this stage he needed a full shot of 50% dextrose to revive him. He was literally in an alcoholic coma. Indeed, with that strong dose of glucose it didn't take long for McAntony to spring back to life and to thank profusely the doctors for recovering him from the jaws of the death, as he later described it. In particular, his old comrade from senate could revive those who had been condemned to death, he always said.

McAntony's incident that night would have ended as quietly as it started in the morning when he received his wages except that the CEO was worried about his position. He was worried that he could be made a scapegoat for all those who had said bad things against the government. He directed the registrar of the university to ensure that serious disciplinary measures were taken against McAntony. The registrar, not wishing to disappoint his boss, convened a disciplinary meeting first thing in the morning. At 7:30 he announced that the head of the department and members of the disciplinary committee should be gathered at his office to dispose of this matter swiftly.

Obviously, McAntony needed to be present for the proceedings to take place. When he arrived, he had brushed himself up, and was literally a transformed individual. Even his beard had been trimmed and he was looking extremely tame and on his best manners. He had even worn an old suit and a pair of shoes; no longer in the paa-pata which he normally used to walk with the open shoes normally people used to go to the bathroom. When the charge against him was read out, his only question was, "Where is it written that because McAntony has gone, feels happy having received his well-earned wages and would deserve to be punished? Where is it written that McAntony cannot express his hard-earned independence of thought and speech when he considers it necessary, even if it is in the middle of the night? Why should the police interfere with his enjoyment of life?"

Obviously the registrar was not in the mood to answer any of those frivolous questions, as he considered them. All he wanted was a summary sentence. When he asked the head of department for his opinion, the head of department was equally philosophical in his approach. He asked the chair of the proceedings, "Mr Registrar, what is the job description of McAntony? Is it not to teach, conduct research and examine and produce young professionals?" Chairman had to concede that was what was described in the job description. Then the head of department went on to ask, "Has McAntony failed to give his lectures?"

Even before anybody could answer, McAntony was ready with an answer. He said, "No, everybody knows that I am the first one to give my marks and I am the first one to be at the graduation ceremony to see my boys and girls off."

Then the head of department continued with the questioning, "Has McAntony failed to conduct research?"

Before anybody else could answer, McAntony jumped in once more he said, "Last year I published 12 scientific papers in those high impact journals. Journals which you, Mr Registrar or

175

your Vice Chancellor can't smell. Show me where your name has appeared," he asked the registrar who opted to ignore the question and the remark about the Vice Chancellor.

Then the head of department continued, "At our department we do not have any issues with McAntony. He is the best academic we have, he's popular with students and he has not failed to deliver. As such, from my point of view, there can be no reason to suspend him as you want us to do. The fact that he proposes to go and ground the secretary general or to bring Arap Moi's government to it is knees is irrelevant to the department. We care that he teaches, he conducts the research and he supports our activities in the community."

Naturally, it was impossible to get a consensus under these circumstances where the head of department was not siding with the management and therefore McAntony escaped with a mere warning, with the provision that should he again bring the institution into disrepute, he would not be only suspended, he would lose his job. As McAntony left, he was pointing to the heavens and with open hands he concluded, "Mr Registrar, don't worry, the old man up there is in charge. It's not you who is in charge." That was the end of the proceedings.

Late that evening McAntony was busy marking examination papers under the moonlight and when passers-by stopped to say hi, he said, "Oh, welcome. We're working hard under the moonlight. The government has disconnected our electricity but yet we must work" and he would draw tick marks; "these students must pass. Clever boys, clever girls, 100%, good answers." On and on he continued to issue marks under the moonlight.

McAntony was one of the strongest supporters of the School of Medicine and its new curriculum. To him, a lot needed to change in the country. He was extremely critical of the attitude of men of the healthcare industry, doctors who only served for a couple of years after graduation before hopping off to open a kiosk in town and making money their lifelong vocation. To him, those they were failures and they were part and parcel of the political class that was short-changing the people of Kenya.

He learned that research had shown that young doctors are likely to go back to their roots if they are trained within the community circumstances that they are familiar with. They identified themselves with the local communities and rural communities away from the city. That in addition to being trained in big city, if from time to time they went into the villages and looked at the state of livelihood, looked at poorly nourished children and understood that one of the reasons that they were malnourished is because the government was exploiting their parents. They would realise that a lot needs to be done and most of it needs to be in the countryside, in the rural areas, in the villages, in the household. In those huts where black smoke was going through the roof.

McAntony did not miss his words in supporting this new revolution and document as he called it. To him, everything including the courses in political science needed to change. Move away from the new text that was now being called, the Nyayo philosophy. Indeed when a proposal was tabled in senate by one of the eminent religious professors with a title, the biblical basis of Nyayo philosophy, McAntony could have hit the dean who brought that kind of document to the enlightened community. "How dare you challenge the word of God? How dare you mix it with the political agenda of the current government? How could you base the philosophy of Arap Moi on the Bible?" he argued.

Peace, love and unity in his view had nothing to do with the Bible. Indeed, he argued extremely eloquently that the church was a source of global disunity, contrary to what this proposal was trying to put across. Needless to say, it was impossible for this proposal to be passed in the senate. Indeed it had to be sent back for change of title. Even if the substance of the study was essentially the same it was in the views of senators not possible to imagine that the existing political philosophy that was being expounded and the way the government was running had a biblical basis.

From time to time, McAntony would come to the school of medicine and give lectures on anthropology as it related to the medical and health practices of the various communities of Kenya. The students found these lectures extremely thought provoking and enlightening. He was the first one to announce that being a university professor did not absolve anybody from succumbing to cultural roots. He even was the first one to give the students statistics to the effect that in the country more than

50% of the population, before they went to seek care in the health facilities, had tried traditional remedies. These included professors like himself.

Therefore in his view there was a need to study indigenous medical practices. Traditional healers needed to be part and parcel of the health provision in the country. Obviously this was not mainstream political thought. It was what you could expect from those fringe groups who thought that western medicine was not necessarily the ideal. He would question, "How come the Chinese are using their own medicine, the Indians are using their own medicine and you guys are telling us to use European medicine?" Needless to say, his ideas and thoughts were thought provoking and ignited some element of curiosity among the young trainees.

McAntony represented a group of professors that strongly supported free thought, free expression and who believed that the youth were the saviours of the nation. In his view they needed to be better prepared, they needed not to be indoctrinated on the basis of the political ideology. They only needed to give any facts and to be shown the ways to analyse facts and to think for themselves. The interaction between McAntony and Salimo always generated laughter and entertainment. When the committee was set up to award bursaries to needy students, he was a natural choice.

When it was the time to deliver it, the results were clear that his views had greatly influenced the outcome. Salimo, the chair of the bursaries committee, valued opinions and ideas not just from those who were popular with the system, but also those who were critical of the system. Indeed, in this instance it was clear that there was need to review and revise the tools for assessing the means assessment that this particular tool was intended to perform. To him and others, it was also clear that tools of this nature had a cultural tinge to them and this cultural tinge needed to be balanced or contextualised, as they argued.

***

With Engineer Kimani there was never a dull moment. Indeed, the combination of Engineer Kimani, Salimo and Charles, to which you could add Orina, was like comedy every day of the week. They had one instance or one story to tell, on a regular basis. Today Engineer Kimani was missing because he had gone on to "To be given evidence". The evidence was an instance where, a passenger in the car was driving had injured himself on the lighting. The story was that usually Engineer Kimani would be coming from his rural home next to the city, and to beat the traffic jam of the city, he had to start at 5:00 AM latest or 4:30 on a regular basis. This is also the time a number of morons from the village of Kajiado would be headed towards Ngong. Engineer Kimani, being a man of the people, never passed any of these morons on the way. He always explained that, who knows, one day they could be his saviour.

Of course what he was alluding to was the frequent hijacking along that route and that he figured out that one of these days he was going to be abandoned in the forest amid the lions and all manner of wild animals and that he was only going to survive because some moron might one come to his aid. Or rather, as he walked back to the highway, he would need someone to rescue him. For that reason, he made a point every time he was driving on that road where there was very little traffic and very few public transport vehicles, to will never pass pedestrians who appeared headed in his direction.

Earlier in the week he had given a ride to one such needy moron. The moron was sitting at the back of his four-wheel base and he was sitting in front with another one. Communication was an issue, but not so much of an issue that the common bond of humanity could be fractured. For that reason acts of charity would be allowed to happen more or less naturally. What the Kamau did not know was where the moron was headed to and where he would get off. As they continued towards the city, the moron next to him signalled him to slow down as they had reached their destination in the middle of nowhere.

As the Land Rover screeched to a halt, the gentleman at the back did not wait for it to completely stop. He preferred to exit so that not too much time is wasted. And on jumping out of the Land Rover, he landed badly, bruising his knee and his elbow. Engineer Kimani came out and inspected and examined him, with his little knowledge of medicine he thought it wasn't too bad. So, he decided to deviate from the highway and drop him at the nearest health clinic. At the clinic the unfortunate passenger was declared perfectly healthy. He only had superficial bruises and was discharged with painkillers.

Only a couple of days later, Engineer Kimani was summoned to appear before the nearest police station to give a statement in a case where he had wilfully caused bodily harm or injury to a passenger by dangerous driving. This was the first time Engineer Kimani would learn that as soon as the moron was declared healthy and fit; outside there was some smart guys, one of them a lawyer, who questioned the moron. He was asked how he came to sustain injuries; on learning that they were a result of a fall from a moving vehicle, the young lawyer informed him that he could earn himself lots of money if he launched a complaint against the driver of this vehicle. So together the moron and the lawyer went to police station and made up the story in a manner that it could serve as a wilful act on the part of the driver. Why else would a disembarking passenger sustain injuries?

Engineer Kimani was flabbergasted when confronted with this act of ungratefulness, as he put it. "Here I was minding my own business and hoping to be a part of humanity, assisting the needy ones and now I'm the one in the dark. The passenger I was trying to assist, he's free and now I'm the one accused of causing injury by dangerous driving." Engineer Kimani then went on to narrate that what saved him was the other moron who was sitting next to him. He explained the incident in great detail, to the satisfaction of the prosecuting officer. In the end, the prosecuting officer concluded that this was a case of ambulance chasers, which some of the lawyers in the city had become. Therefore, he opted to drop any further charges against Engineer Kimani.

Engineer Kimani in his narration, declared that never again, would he stop to give a lift to a moron who is minding his own business. If he had minded his own business, he would have been at the station on time. But as it was, he was now having to defend his reputation and to save himself from a hefty fine. As was usually the case, one story led to another and it provoked Charles to narrate a similar incidence, but under different circumstances. According to Charles, the story he was telling originated from McAntony himself.

McAntony had, on having been released, arguably, given pattern from these transgressions. You never, never, never give up the idea that the politicians need to be changed, and therefore, whatever instance, whenever there was an issue involving a politician, particularly with negative consequences, McAntony would magnify it tenfold. In this case, he was telling a story of that politician whom he had vowed to trounce during the forthcoming election. McAntony was peddling a story about how that politician was involved in a scandalous incidence and that he was due to appear in court. According to McAntony, the politician was in the company of one of his advisers, one of whom decided to take time out. Unknown to them, he had decided to go off to a rural town for a weekend in the company of a young lady. The story goes that the young lady was now being accused of murder.

The young lady, when asked what happened in the moments before the demise of the late adviser, narrated events of the day in great detail. That having been out for the whole evening, they were in bed and little did she know that this gentlemen was suffering from one condition or another. All she knew was that it was at one moment in time, he appeared to be in pain which was interpreted as pleasure until suddenly he had a convulsion from which he never gained consciousness. Obviously, this became a matter of police investigation, of course it was a case of sudden death. Charles would not let Orina complete the story that McAntony was peddling. "You mean this man died in action?"

"Well, so to say," Orina went on.

When asked to relay the circumstances, the young lady explained to the investigating officer, that as far as she could tell he was mumbling something to the effect of, "My god, I'm coming." She interpreted this to be a pre-orgasmic expression and she went on to say, little did she know that what he meant by, "My god I'm coming" was him actually announcing his intentions to check out! As far as she was concerned, she didn't have anything to do with this event. She was just minding her own business when the gentleman gave up the ghost. A post-mortem examination was due to be conducted. And upon the outcome of this examination the fate of the young lady would be decided. Therefore, the group concluded, sometime it's better to mind your own business and let others carry their own cross.

In recognition of McAntony but more so, his compatriot professor who prematurely died, one grateful student composed and recited the following poetic piece:

The learned professor read and read all the books to be read; Professor read every book that was ever written on the subject;
The professor read each line and between the lines of every page of the book; Professor read books forwards and backwards!
The learned professor wrote many books; Professor wrote on every blank page;
Professor wrote even on pages that were already written upon; Professor wrote books from front and from the back
The learned professor will be much missed for he checked out prematurely!

This was the time when young academicians were falling prey to HIV/AIDS epidemic in the country.

***

"The professor is extremely well learned," one day an elderly gentleman who exuded great wisdom was explaining to his friends.

"His education is immense," he continued.

To illustrate the extent of the professor's learning, the old man stated, "his schooling extends from the tip of my fingers to the top of my shoulder," he continued, with his arm fully extended to well above the his head.

"But his foolishness is equally immense," the old man continued.

To demonstrate how immense, he once more used his still-stretched arm, "his foolishness extends as from my shoulder to the tip of my fingers," lowering his arm deep towards the ground.

In so doing the old man gave a summation of the learning equation whose net result was zero!

This was an elderly gentleman assessing one of the senior professors at Salimo's university.

The analysis was born of arguments and counter arguments on a number of social development projects that would have been initiated by a church group but remained undone because of infighting and wrangling.

This was about McAntony, one of Salimo's good friends at the university. Little did the elderly gentleman know; Salimo, who was now riding in the same car, knew the professor. It could also be that the speaker was passing a message.

And so was his colleague McAntony, who was one of the most brilliant minds in the republic. The only one who could explain and describe in great detail, the origin and times of earlier forms of human beings in the republic.

McAntony was eccentric in some ways. In one way he was unable to reconcile with the ruling class, as he called them. Then, he never saw eye to eye with any of the ideas of the regime in power. To him this was a road to hell; the question was, at what point do we believe that we are now in hell. He led one of the most important organizations in the republic before he crossed swords with the leaders and was let go.

It was not difficult for him to get his direct route into academia. In any case, in academia you can hold potentially conflicting views and opinions and yet you can work together productively. In many cases this conflict of views, is in itself, in many instances, the building block for better and more productive ideas. Now, in class McAntony was an excellent and exceptional teacher, he identified with students, which too often is the case with extremely eccentric professors.

He was most popular with students and well liked. He was down to earth in all ways; his mode of dressing, his mode of presentation and his views about how students would learn and what they should learn. In senate he was a very strong debater, always standing for the facts, standing for what is right and standing for his own beliefs.

From time to time he would throw punches at the medical faculty. For example, would say, "Will the people from the medical faculty join us the humans." Humans meaning, those from the faculty of humanities. From time to time he would come with extremely useful phrases and ideas which would make one think twice before even saying anything. For example, when the chair was adamant in giving people deadlines, McAntony would say, "No, no, no, sir. I don't think a deadline is good for them. Let us throw them a lifeline." That would change the entire mood of discussion in the senate.

Unfortunately, the parents and the public in general least appreciated these cranky professors who would be rowdy when they are sober and even noisier when they have drunk one bottle too many. Indeed, a group of villagers who came to witness the graduation ceremony of their daughter, the only one from the village, were shocked when, while the names were being read out, a section of the crowd of students started cheering and clapping.

When they turned round there was this rough looking gentleman, with a long beard, tinged eyes, and in flip-flops, coming for graduation. Obviously, for the parents, who had travelled hundreds of miles to come and witness the graduation of their beloved daughter, there was extreme incongruence between the occasion and the man who was being cheered.

When they enquired they were told that is the great McAntony. Well-liked by students, not so well liked by the university, often unwelcome to the public gallery. For many days to come the village team never stopped commenting about this intellectual giant who appeared from nowhere and caused hysteria in the graduation ceremony.

"Hey, how are you doing, doc?" It was McAntony who had arrived at the bank and as usual he had something to say to the medic. He said, "It is good to see our wages."

"Why do you think so?"

"Because it could have been worse," he said. "We may not have had our pay this month, and thank God."

***

"This regime is an oligarchy of kleptomaniacs," declared Alberto, with such a finality that they dared not question this view. This was in reference to the Moi regime, which by then had been in power for a quarter of a century.

"His are not Cabinet Ministers but 'Captains of Misery'!" he concluded.

Alberto was prone to making off the cuff pronouncements that left friend and foe stupefied.

"It is impossible to hide an elephant under a strawberry tree," he challenged those who dared accuse his country's apparent domineering role.

***

Salimo's meeting with Alberto was purely coincidental but a most fortunate event. Alberto was born in Switzerland; the last born to a family of five. In five generations of his family he was the only one who did not become a lawyer; a crime for which he paid dearly. "My father, then chief of the justice department in the republic could not accept deviation from the family tradition," Alberto explained to them one day as they enjoyed their office lunch of roasted maize.

"When I announced that I wanted to be a doctor," Alberto continued, "my father communicated to the family that Alberto would have to pay for himself through college if he wanted to be a doctor!"

"With that pronouncement, my fate was sealed, setting me on the long and strenuous road through medical school," concluded Alberto.

This was long after Alberto senior had the budding doctor arrested for forging his signature so he could train as a pilot. The law required that to be issued with a licence to train as a pilot one had to be at least seventeen years old. Alberto had forged a letter to the training school purporting to be from his father confirming that his son was eighteen years old and had his permission to train as a pilot. As the chief of the justice department, nobody would doubt the letter and Alberto was duly enrolled as a trainee pilot.

As fate would have it, Alberto and his classmates did not know that they would be soaring high above the golf course where his father and a colleague were on their first hole. On hearing and spotting the trainer plane, his friend had casually remarked, "That must be my son and Alberto, in that plane." The name Alberto only registered at the second hole.

Turning to his friend he enquired, "Which Alberto is training with your son?"

"Your son, Alberto, yes, Alberto is training together with my son," his friend continued, without noticing the profound effect the words had on the older man.

"That cannot be him, my son is hardly seventeen," he retorted as he abandoned the game and headed for the nearest telephone.

Alberto only knew something was wrong when he saw his father at the end of the runway as he was taxiing in to a stop. The old man was not alone. The manager of the training school, the head of the city police department and a couple of soldiers were there. No sooner had Alberto's feet touched the holy ground than the nearest officer snapped the handcuffs on his poor hands.

"And with that my lessons were abruptly and dramatically put on hold for the next twelve months," announced Alberto with a mischievous smile.

To call Alberto now a qualified physician and a rebel is to understate the man. During his medical studies, he volunteered for every paying research work. Not as a researcher but as a subject for testing!

"This was so much fun, I mean as the guinea pig," Alberto declared.

"Yes, I participated even for the psychotropic drugs like marijuana," he continued, to their amazement.

"And I think I am a better doctor and researcher," he informed the novices!

This was one of those days when Alberto talked as if possessed by seismic inspiration. They had been to a meeting of the damn donors. The American had talked as if without donor support the sun would stop rising in Kenya.

"There has to be evidence of real commitment from the government," warned the outspoken American representative.

Alberto called her the "American piglet" for she was bursting through the seams. There was also the "Kenyan piglet" and the "World Bank piglet".

"First they have to stop stealing from their people," echoed the "viper".

The "viper" was the lady from Sweden who saw thieves in every government office, corridor or car park. In her view everywhere one turned, there was a government official waiting to steal something anytime! Every time she opened her mouth a stinger escaped.

The day before this meeting, the papers had carried a story on how the Minister for Health had skimmed off five million dollars.

The Kenyan piglet had tried in vain to wish the allegation off but the foul air had poisoned the meeting beyond redemption. And so, together with Alberto, they had left in time for lunch, not at their regular Chinese restaurant, but in the office. Once a week they would let off the cholesterol by eating roasted maize. Today was one such a day. While Ndungu the driver went to the roadside roasters, they passed the time through small talk.

On this particular day there was also to be a special event; Olof Kjaer the Swede in their office was going for home leave. Later in the day they would be bidding him goodbye. Ole Sagini and the Dane, who reigned on the purse strings, had secured one bottle of brandy for the occasion.

The afternoon went much faster than they thought and using water glasses, Sagini poured the hissing drink for the six of them in the office.

One month later, Olof Kjaer arrived from Nankoping, cursing, "You bastards almost killed me."

Working with Alberto was like studying obstetrics with Professor Gebbie. Gebbie was born premature. "Through the marvels of medicine and technology, I survived imminent death, I grew to become a professor!" he would marvel every time he talked about pregnancy and birth.

One day the subject was contraceptive technology.

"There are two principle methods for avoiding pregnancy," Gebbie introduced the subject. "One is the metal can method and the other is the aspirin method," he announced. "Do you know the can method?" He questioned each of them in turn and in each case elicited negative response.

"I knew you would not know this," he continued to explain with the ever-mischievous look on his face!

"The aspirin method is the one that virgins practice. The woman place one aspirin tablet between her thighs and keeps it in position throughout the night. In this way the man has no chance of getting near anywhere near the love bud or G-spot," as he usually referred to the female organs. When he was teaching

187

pregnancy and labour, he called it the birth canal. When he taught them gynaecology or issues of sexuality, he preferred the term love bud to differentiate between sensual feelings of the latter as opposed to the vegetative process in birth! "In medicine we call this the abstinence method."

The whole class broke into wild laughter at this characterisation of abstinence!

To them aspirin had another connotation; that of analgesia, lack of feelings, no sensation! Picture the pea-sized aspirin held between the thighs of a woman for easily twelve hours! This was also evidence based: the aspirin would be in position on checking in the morning!

"The metal can method is the one my wife and I practise," Gebbie continued without any mirth. "You see, my wife is about six feet tall and I am only five plus a few inches. So when we make love, we do it standing. Because of my height I stand on the metal can. We have a metal can about six inches tall, the one that you normally buy from the supermarket containing five kilograms of cooking oil. The idea is that when my wife notes that I have started to have nystagmus or that my eyes are rolling round like those of a chameleon, she kicks the can from under my feet and I drop with a thud. This is called the withdrawal method!"

The ensuing laughter in the class could be heard in the dean's office leading to the dean herself paying the class a visit soon thereafter. Of course not even the ever-amiable Gebbie would dare explain the meaning of the laughter. The dean was easily some inches above six feet and had the deepest voice on campus.

The students loved Gebbie.

It was not the sense of humour he emanated. In one statement he delivered multiple messages. For example, in the dramatization of the aspirin and the metal can methods: for the method to work both parties must actively participate. Sex has to be negotiated and this requires self-discipline. The technical requirements of the methods were so demanding that usually these methods, though the cheapest and simplest to execute (not using the metal can), were the least used and least successful!

"Abstinence is one hundred percent protective of pregnancy and venereal diseases while withdrawal has no protective properties and the failure rate is about thirty percent," Gebbie concluded the lecture.

***

Salimo's four years as 'permanent casual worker', as Alberto referred to Salimo was a revelation on the rot in Moi government. Anything that could be stolen was stolen.

"This is no longer Afya House," declared Alberto one morning. "It is Mafia House," he continued. This was before he dropped the 'a' at the end of Mafia to give the house the foulest description. This was said on the day there was no water in the office block and the toilets gave a foul smell, all the way from lower ground floor to the seventh floor!

The mandarins in the Ministry were always plotting on how to skim off something. It was in Salimo's second year when he came face-to-face with the scandal of the year. On this day his friend Naimara had been served with a dismissal letter. That he would be dismissed was no secret because Naimara's tongue was lighter than paper but sharper than a razor blade. He would not spare anybody big or small. One day he jibed at President Moi, "Sir, with due respect, your government is full of thieves". On another day he telephoned the Netherlands Ambassador to complain.

"Your Excellency, why does your country send us thieves?" Naimara demanded. "This man selling us X-ray machines is a thief... yes, he wants to steal from the Kenyan Government!" he continued, between puffs of his favourite cigarette. The sales manager had inflated the prices of X-ray machines and equipment.

The sales manager, who had been listening to this conversation, was both red and sweating from head to toe. He had by now stopped recalculating the numbers, sensing an explosive situation. The man was called back to the Embassy, never to return to Kenya, at least on a similar mission.

"Professor," he called Salimo "These pigs want to fire me but they will fail," he announced emphatically.

It was during this time at Mafia House that Salimo attempted to strike at the heart of the cancer of corruption, a one-man effort that was doomed to fail. It was also at the same station where he truly understood how evil the blackest heart is, as Naimara called it. Cruel would be a more befitting description.

Naimara had discovered a scheme involving senior government officials that would not only divert millions of dollars from a World Bank funded project but one that could also have infected thousands of health workers and security personnel with HIV by administering a contaminated hepatitis B vaccine.

One million doses had arrived at the Jomo Kenyatta Airport, without any form of certification or observance of the most fundamental requirements for cold storage, either in transit or at the port of entry. Naimara had merely been instructed to clear the goods and arrange for payment.

Smelling a rotten rat, Naimara enlisted the assistance of Salimo. "Professor," as he referred to Salimo, "this is strange!"

"There is no documentation to show when and who ordered the vaccine," he confided in Salimo.

A quick check on the pricing showed that the vaccine was costing a tenth of the actual cost of the newly introduced genetically produced vaccine that had replaced the serum-derived product.

Naimara and Salimo recommended to the Ministry of Health to send samples to South Africa for analysis as Kenya did not have the new generation methods of testing that involved actual identification of DNA to see if any virus proteins were in the vaccine. Even more importantly the simple question that needed to be answered was; is this product truly the crystalline version that is genetically manufactured, as the sources industry claimed on the package?

However, before the necessary authorisation could be given (it was unclear if indeed this was going to be given), Salimo would learn while outside the country and from anonymous sources, that that particular batch was due for disposal somewhere in Belgium but there was no evidence that the procedures were followed through according to the law. The sources informed Salimo that a senior company representative in Nairobi working in consort with senior government officials conspired to cash in on the vaccine.

An order was clandestinely made to the laboratory that was required to destroy the vaccine to divert the entire consignment to Kenya to help save the lives of the at-risk professionals identified as health workers and the security forces.

Armed with this information, Salimo prepared a detailed technical report for the Office of the President, the Ministry of Health and the Army Commander. But not being sure if all these offices would take any action or indeed if the executive agencies could be absolved from the scam, he embarked on documented action – firstly from the chief executive of the Ministry of Health to embargo the consignment and by making a face-to-face presentation to the security chiefs.

Despite these determined efforts, it was not possible to prevent the government from paying for the full cost of this worthless and potentially lethal product. Worse still, soon thereafter, Naimara and the Chief Executive of the Ministry of Health were summarily dismissed and leaving the Chief Medical Officer at liberty to "dispose" of the vaccine.

The matter gravitated into the long catalogue of this and many similar government misappropriations contained in the Auditor General's report that is usually four to five years late!

This and many similar failed attempts to take a terminal and lethal stab at corruption did not deter Salimo from joining a group of young professionals from taking their crusade to the very heart of government – the Presidency.

"My son, tell me who is at the heart of this corruption in the Ministry of Health?" the President enquired with genuine concern.

On learning the name of the culprit, the President took a long sigh and looking Salimo in the face and with abject resignation, quipped, "If I remove him, the entire Kikuyu community will descend, accusing my government of finishing them!"

Professionally, Salimo thought of himself a man of the world or more accurately, a nomad – one time at the horn of Africa and another time at the opposite pole of the continent. The four years in Asmara were in one sense highly productive but at the same time a bit of a waste of one's productive life.

The Special Assistant to the Secretary General summarised a foreigner's life in Eritrea in one sentence, "Surely Asmara must be the only city in the entire world where you can die on Friday only for your body to be discovered on Monday morning and the post-mortem will be unequivocal in its findings that the cause of death was absolute boredom."

The School Project went smoothly, thanks to the foreign contingent professors. The students were great; as malleable as copper wire. Did they have a choice? The regime in power assured absolute acquiescence, or so Salimo felt.

He had witnessed the "vanishing" of Dr Fustum, the only trained psychiatrist in the entire state of Eritrea. Doubling as priest counsellor and advisor to the School Management, he posed a threat to the regime through association with the enemies of the regime. He even dared admonish his flock to stand up for their rights.

Receiving donation of any kind – monetary or material – from foreign agencies was enough evidence that you were hostile to the state. Fustum committed the double sin against the state, one of being close to God and the second of being close to foreign agents.

A foreign envoy who dared call for opening the space for dialogue found himself on the state-run bus from Massawa to the airport. To Salimo, this was the very personification of a rogue regime.

In this country, life had come to standstill for most of the people. Motion was dangerous to the state. Space belonged to the regime. Space would give way to motion. Motion would emancipate.

To another envoy who dared call for more food aid to the starving peasants, the rebuke was both quick in coming and bellicose: "You foreigners! Why should you be more Catholic than the pope!"

"The four years in Asmara was a much more powerful potion than any lesson on the importance of the four freedoms; particularly the freedoms of movement and free thought," declared Salimo, upon completion of his tour of duty, as he called it.

It was in Asmara where Salimo learnt that cheap things can be costly. This had happened to his comrade Prof Jairus Mpofu who had travelled on a cheap air ticket to Johannesburg. The total fare was four hundred American dollars for a return ticket!

But there was a catch to it. You transited at Sanaa. What this meant was that when you were outbound you spent one night in the capital of Yemen at a hotel of the airline's choice. Prof Mpofu narrated his ordeal upon return.

"Salimo," he bemoaned, "we had beans for breakfast, beans for lunch and beans for dinner." As if that was not enough, he continued, "I had just dropped off to sleep when there was a knock my hotel room door."

"Who is there?" I asked.

"Room service, we have brought your roommate."

Even without waiting for Prof Mpofu to open the door, the escort yanked the door open and in came "a cigar-chomping American traveller, most likely from Texas," narrated Prof Mpofu.

"How do you do mate!" rang out the greeting.

"Great!" responded Prof Mpofu as he bade farewell to his sleep.

"Salimo, I was reminded of my first day in New York when I went to a store to arm myself with a few cans of Heineken for the night," he continued.

"As I turned around the aisle with the beers, I chanced on a not too well groomed heavyweight who was running his fingers down each side of a scary looking machete – to test its sharpness.

"The heavyweight, without even looking at me, quipped, 'What is up?'

"My entire body was seized by terror; as I turned the corner to flee; the six-can pack crashed with a thunderous noise and suddenly each can seem to have grown three legs as they rang out in different directions!

"Now in this hotel room, I had this misfortune of sharing a room with the unwelcome guest!

"How could I sleep? I was not even sure what his sexual orientation might be!

"As if this was not enough, on my return leg, there was a sand storm over Sanaa Airport and we had to divert to Aden.

"Unfortunately by the time the sky cleared and we were allowed to land at Sanaa, my flight to Asmara had left, which meant one more night in the same hotel.

"Salimo, I used all my powers of persuasion to negotiate my return to Dubai! Better pay a little more than face imminent death in the hotel room!"

"Cheap can be expensive!" he concluded. To Salimo, Asmara was the perfect place where to appreciate life for what it is, uncomplicated and pure. The air was clean and security was excellent, with little or no communication with the outside world. Anything that could run out did run out. Here you had time to think about the past, the present and the future. The country was in a state of no war and yet no peace. Therefore travel was limited. Moreover, the many permits required to travel from one city to the other were enough deterrent. He felt freed from the cares of politics; there was only one ruling class, the military. Everybody else was dispensable. More and more frequently he remembered the old days in the medical school.

Asmara was the perfect place to apply his clinical acumen. The Professor of Psychiatry would have found practising here the challenge that medical practice is meant to be. There was not too much technology to go by. Your five senses were all that mattered.

"Learn to listen to the patient," was the cardinal rule, as Muhanji called it. To prove his case, one day he arrived in class with several metres of electrocardiogram readings from a patient. "Boys and girls, look at this great waste of resources," he remonstrated, letting the tape run along the entire side of the room.

"The blinking physicians could have saved themselves a lot of time and the patient a lot of money if they had listened more to the patient than themselves!" Muhanji then went on to explain to the class how anxiety mimics many heart conditions. This patient complained of palpitations. He appeared tense and had recently been suspended from his job over misappropriated funds in his office.

"Gentlemen, Asmara is paradise," their boss would remind them whenever, their complaints threatened to boil over. "If only you knew what we went through in Sierra Leone during and immediately after the coup after they murdered Siaka Stevens."

One day, with his eyes watering, he, Andrew, narrated how he cheated death the day after the coup, saved by members of the militia who objected to his decapitation, citing his generosity. Unknown to him, he had offered some members of the junta a few dollars to buy themselves a warm meal at the end of a particularly long official engagement.

The President had rewarded him with a Deputy Minister's post in return for his loyalty and services as the personal physician. He was made the Deputy Minister for Health.

All was not lost on this cheap excursion ticket. More surprises were awaiting Salimo about this fateful journey. Prof Mpofu then continued his tale on how, upon landing, he chanced to meet a colleague right at the airport. Unknown to him, the friend was now a deputy minister.

In manner of saying halloo, Prof Mpofu asked "Doc, what are you doing here?"

"How you are you and what are you doing here?" replied Prof Mpofu's old friend from the medical school.

Prof Mpofu replied, "It could be better. How are you today?"

The discussion would have gone on the small talk level but Professor Mpofu turned to more pressing matters of arranging for transport to town. On his part the Deputy complained with irritation, "These guys do not keep time!"

Soon Prof Mpofu waved down the manager who promptly and profusely apologised before he proceeded to empty a sizeable package of local currency in exchange for one hundred dollars.

Not wanting to take anything for granted, Prof Mpofu proceeded to invite his old friend to accompany him downtown in the hired taxi.

Once both men were in the taxi, lively conversation ensued between the two former associates. "Where should I drop you in town?" Prof Mpofu asked.

The Deputy Minister retorted, "Is that how you talk to a Minister?"

Prof Mpofu was bewildered with amusement and irritation and asked, "Which Minister?"

"Don't you know that I am now the new Deputy Minister for health?" his compatriot replied.

"Don't you read these things in the newspapers?"

The Deputy Minister continued as Prof Mpofu looked at him with an open mouth and a rueful smile but without saying anything.

Prof Mpofu: "Frankly, I don't read the news and, Mr Minister I am not interested."

"And is that how you deal with the black market?" The Deputy Minister had asked as a matter of course, not expecting an answer.

Prof Mpofu reminded himself that he was a passenger in this car, minister or no minister. Prof Mpofu said, "By the way, Mr Minister, what are you doing to our country? How do you expect people in this country to survive? Have you no feelings?"

Deputy Minister: "To be honest things are tough."

Prof Mpofu resignedly replied, "But what do you expect with people like you, our role model, running away to Australia?"

Prof Mpofu then learnt that in the meantime prices had risen exponentially and for example, the price of bread had risen 300 times in the space of one week. Gasoline was only available on payment in foreign currency. As for the quality of bread: it was 80% maize-meal, 2% wheat, and the rest was water and salt.

The next morning Prof Mpofu had left his residence while indicating that he would be returning for lunch.

"Which lunch?" was the quick response from the house girl. "The people are slowly withering away!"

The trip back to Asmara was not any better; two days at Sanaa in Yemen was the icing on the cake. It was beans for breakfast, beans for lunch and beans for dinner! At one moment Professor Mpofu had reacted to one brand of beans and was sore all over his body. The return trip was equally long. While approaching Sanaa Airport, landing had to be aborted due to a severe sand storm. The flight was diverted to Aden.

"Another round of the deadly beans!" Professor Mpofu lamented.

"No way," the professor told himself. Better pay for a connection back at Dubai than risk instant death.

***

Soon the young doctor was now not working for the government or anybody in particular. His name was O'Masaii, a name that he was proud of. He had trained as a surgeon.

He had now resigned from the government service and was not in a hurry to be enslaved, as he often referred to any kind of long-term formal employment.

"I am now an occupational nomad," he would introduce himself.

"I no longer cut human beings: I cut paper," was now a familiar addition whenever he was introduced to an audience that raised eyebrows as if asking "what is a surgeon doing here?" or quizzical eyes would be saying, "Excuse me: does this place look like a theatre?" He had just arrived at Entasopia to carry out an evaluation of the Trachoma project being run by the village people themselves. They were referred to as the Trachoma monitors.

"It is not funny," he thought. "This country spends lots and lots of scarce money to train health personnel whom it cannot employ. They then spend still more money to train lay people to run the health services for the poor!"

"Ours is two countries in one," he thought.

"One country for the rich and the other for the poor," he lamented.

"My name is Masaii," he thought, wondering if his parents had had a premonition that he would one day work with the Maasai people.

He had had a long day.

He had been interviewing the bishop of the Catholic diocese.

"It is not my job to convert the Maasai from their way of worshipping God or their religion and make Catholics out of them," the bishop had concluded.

"Why did this man of God leave his country if he did not intend to make any disciples for Jesus?" the young doctor wondered.

In some ways, he and the bishop were alike.

"Probably, the Maasai have a more profound understanding of God than us who try to evangelise them," the bishop had emphatically concluded.

"My vocation is to assist the Maasai people improve their living conditions," explained the bishop.

"We build schools for them, train them on how grow food and avoid disease," the bishop continued as they walked through one of the new hospitals.

Many things struck the doctor. The hospital was very large; too large for the community it served. The architecture was

Italian. It was hot inside: too hot for anybody to carry out any serious clinical work.

The surgeon was also struck by the fact that there were no patients. The wards were empty and there was only one pregnant woman waiting to be seen by the Italian doctor. "The Maasai men do not allow women to feed them or treat them," the Italian doctor explained.

"Worse still, no moron worth his salt eats alone," she continued. "That is why our wards are empty," the head nurse added.

There were many thoughts in the surgeon's mind. He wondered why there were so many contradictions in the practice of medicine in his country.

Here is a man of God who does not believe in converting the Maasai people to his religion. He wants to improve their living conditions. He has brought the Hollywood ambience into the heart of Maasailand – a hospital that almost nobody uses.

The rest of the projects the diocese was involved in were truly remarkable. In particular the micro-credit scheme for the women had impressed the surgeon.

One group of women struck the surgeon as not only ingenious, but though unable to read or write, well versed in fundamental concepts of commerce.

One of the women was especially vocal and could not restrain her disdain for the ignorant economists the church had employed to manage the scheme.

She wanted the surgeon to explain why the so-called economists could not understand why the women should pay their loans as one instalment at the end of the year. "Ask him," she demanded through the interpreter, "why they continue to escalate the repayment every month when we default when they know very well that we sell our produce only once a year?"

The surgeon was now reflecting on the encounter with the members of the women group. These women understood the principles of compound interest without ever going to school.

"They understood elements of return on investment better than me!" the surgeon said loudly.

This particular group would invest the loan in livestock. They bought calves and reared them for twelve to eighteen months before selling them at a huge profit. With this income, they would make one repayment.

Unfortunately, the project was designed to have monthly loan repayments and if they defaulted, they compounded the interest, which eroded their margin of profit.

He remembered the words of his friend Alberto, "Jesus did not attend any formal schooling but is an un-paralleled scholar."

"It is you, the so-called learned who cheat and exploit the masses," Alberto would bitterly add.

The surgeon pondered long into the night over the events of the day. "Here are real people with real problems and real solutions," he thought. His life as a surgeon was worthwhile but not challenging. There is only one way of opening into the abdomen or the head. Once you mastered this all was routine. He considered the surgeon's life to be one of drudgery and a sure way to ignominy and poverty.

"Why should anybody have respect for a person who sticks their fingers up their rectum?" his colleague wondered.

That night the surgeon understood that this was his calling: to live and work among the people.

***

"Massie dear, you shouldn't think of things like having a mission in life," Angelika admonished.

"Massie" had become the pet name for the surgeon among close friends.

The surgeon was whining about life; its meaning, and whether one could go through life without leaving behind any discernible mark.

"That is leading a purely vegetative life," the surgeon lamented.

"Do you know that you can grow a complete human being from one cell taken from the skin?" asked Masaii.

Undeterred, Angel continued to remonstrate with him.

"To dream of a mission in life is too lofty and preparing for disappointment," she warned him.

Her name was Angelika but Masaii preferred to call her "Angel".

"I am hardly a model of anything, let alone an angel," she would protest.

Masaii and Angelika had met in London and almost instantaneously hit it off together. She was recently separated from her husband.

"Two lonely souls" is how Charles explained the relationship.

"Lonely souls seek each other out and stick together like, *chandana Sagini*," Charles announced to the pair.

He used the figurative Swahili expression about the ring and the finger.

In real time experiences the six months they were seeing each other was more than a lifetime of living together. If they were not working, they would be in the theatre to watch the latest play, or rummaging through the big stores in Oxford Street.

"Come and see something wonderful from your country," Angelika excitedly pulled Masaii to an exclusive corner in the store marked "Tana Lawn".

"This is the finest cotton in the world," explained Angelika, "and it comes from your country," she continued.

Judging by the price of the products, the surgeon concluded that yes, indeed, this was very special cotton. Only that until today, he heard had not heard of Tana Lawn, let alone cotton from Tana.

"It must be coming from somewhere near river Tana," he thought, as he ran his finger through the fabric.

They spent some of the time together travelling. Ireland reminded him of Limuru in Kenya.

They visited some ancient ruins in Ireland where the small lakes had some of the clearest waters in the world. The water was so clear, it was like a mirror. Masaii spent hours poring over the water, taking photographs of the reflections off the water, showing the perfect symmetry of the objects.

The visit to the Museum of Torture in Amsterdam was a revelation into Europe's dark past.

"Have you ever heard of 'putting on the rack' or 'turning on the screws'?" asked Angelika. To Masaii until now, these were mere expressions from the English language. He did not know that they held concrete meaning, being derived from the instruments of torture used by the ancestors of the queens and kings of the European empires!

Masaii had just returned from a conference on torture held in Copenhagen where he had spent long hours listening to the escapees from the South American tyranny. During some of the sessions they had relived the psychological torture. He heard of torture by electrical current applied to the birth canal or the use of the balloon in the intestines. Based on the surgeon's knowledge of biology, these would be some of the most painful experiences!

Many of the escapees were from Argentina while some were from Turkey. But regardless of their country of origin, they all had one thing in common: pain in the eyes. Yes, it was pain, not bitterness.

"Look at me," Angelika complained, as they were having coffee after the visit to the Museum of Torture.

"I am a miserable example of a married woman," Angelika managed between her sobbing.

"Never call me angel, please..." she pleaded, as she tightly hugged her love.

She was sensing the separation that was now inevitable as Masaii was leaving for Kenya. "I hate separation," she continued to sob.

Masaii did not know how to console Angelika and could only kiss her on the lips. "You stole something from me," she continued as she regained her usual composure.

"What?" Masaii asked.

"You stole love from my heart," she replied as she gave him the last hug. "Look at that sculpture," Angelika cajoled.

"That is you, my dear," she explained.

Masaii laughed at the wooden sculpture. It was a naked black man. "His behind is little too generous," Masaii joked.

"If it will remind you of me then that is fine with me," he continued as he stroked her chin and ran his hand through her soft hair.

***

With each passing day, Masaii sensed there was a real possibility that he would go through life without achieving anything, but he never lost hope. From the day he announced that scientists could grow a complete replica of person using one skin cell, he understood that he would achieve his mission in life. He wasn't sure what his mission would be. But he was sure a man does not go through life like walking through the sand in the desert or like a bird flying through the air, leaving no trace on its path. He had taken to frequently praying to God to give him a hint or to bless his endeavours so he could leave his mark somewhere in the universe.

"When you want something, the entire universe conspires in helping you to achieve it." He had recently read this in Paul Coelho's novel, *The Alchemist*.

He was now 37 years old and was still not sure whether he had a mission in life or would spend the next thirty, forty or fifty years just waiting to die. He understood the anguish that Julius Caesar was going through on discovering that he was approaching the third decade of his life without an empire to his name while at eighteen Sagini the Great was already a King!

Lately he had converted to meditation.

He would spend precisely thirty minutes between noon and half past twelve meditating. It was not difficult for him to throw his lot with the visiting practitioners of meditation. The couple was very dedicated and appeared concerned about the welfare of mankind. They repeatedly asserted that if only five percent of the about one million inhabitants of Nairobi devoted half an hour each day to meditation, the city would be tranquil and there would be no need for a police force, let alone poor people in want.

At first each session of meditation provided him with the tranquillity that his heart yearned for. His was a restless heart. On a previous occasion, his colleagues – doctors, nurses and staff in theatre were left speechless as he expounded on his theory on why some people succeed while others don't. The difference, he emphatically announced, was that "Those who succeed have a restless heart. They will not rest at anything until they obtain some results. A genius is one who goes the extra mile or remains awake a moment longer when the others have given in to sleep."

Before he joined the meditation class, he had spent agonising days, wondering if his heart was not too restless and he might die prematurely of some heart ailment.

He did not want his to be a life of a blinking physician. He had vowed not to succumb to this wasted life. He had seen too many of the senior doctors working their hearts out before becoming alcoholic wrecks or acquiring a second mistress from the bar. He was recently haunted by the prophecy, or was it a warning, from one of their professors. "Most of you will marry nurses or bar girls," the professor had announced. "Doctors either marry nurses or bar girls!"

Masaii understood that if your heart is not restless you settle for familiar circumstances. How else would the choice for doctors be so limited to these two options? If he had closed his eyes as directed during the time of receiving his *manthra*, he might as well have wound up his practice and joined the great teachers of meditation, dedicating his life to healing through this means and not the use of the scalpel.

He was curious about what was going to happen, so instead of closing his eyes as directed, he watched the proceedings.

While one of the teachers was chanting some words, the lady went around confiding in each of them their individual *manthra*. When she approached him he closed his eyes to receive the magical word.

The lights were switched off and the room completely dark except for the candle that burned at the end of the hall.

Masaii questioned the difference between this ritual and that of a cult or what was said of Free Masons. He felt uncomfortable and frightened.

"This cannot be the way to my mission," he thought.

***

Thursday and Saturday were his best days at work. On Thursday, he drove himself to the Mission hospital deep down at the bottom of the Rift Valley. The drive was through some of the most picturesque parts of the country. When he was alone, which was most of the time, his spirit was renewed from the silence all around him. Occasionally he came across another motorist and they waved at each other – lonely travellers. Most often it was cattle grazing by the roadside and many goats.

The three hours to the hospital were the best time to think while gently stepping on the gas. The car from the missionaries responded well, as if not wanting to distract her master. These were the shortest three hours anywhere on this earth, was his usual complaint. He would immediately correct himself; the three hours back on Saturday morning were the shortest.

On arrival, Sister GM, as she was known, was at hand to receive the surgeon.

Sister GM always insisted on giving him a body hug. She would then hand him over to the senior nurse or visiting doctor to lead him to the patients to be operated on the following day.

Once they had settled the cases, which would be around five in the evening, they would all sit together in the convent house for tea and cakes.

Sister GM would be serving the tea and passing around the cakes.

Very soon it would be dinnertime and Sister GM would lead him to his room a few doors away from her own room.

For three years the surgeon settled into this routine.

"Maybe this is my mission," he wondered on some occasions. On other occasions he would consider these a mere diversion from the main mission of his life, which he did not know yet.

Opening people's abdomens or hammering metal into the bone marrow to fix some nasty fracture cannot be anybody's mission. If you have done a good job even the scar is soon healed and the patient has forgotten the pain. This is why the surgeon insisted on transverse incisions and a stitch that remained under the skin. The healing was perfect and there was no ugly scar to remind the patient.

Unfortunately his approach was not very popular with the nursing staff, particularly when performing caesarean section. The nurses preferred the incision along the abdomen. It was much quicker to get to the womb and even more so to fix everything back.

"A woman is not bread," he would protest.

Masaii would then proceed to administer the anaesthesia to the spine before scrubbing. The extraction of the baby was normally quite fast. He would aim at no more than ten minutes although spinal anaesthesia was much safer than the inhalational or general anaesthesia.

After the mother had been shown her baby and the baby had been handed over to the midwife, the surgeon would then meticulously fix the skin stitch which was often one along the cut. After five days the nurse pulled the thread from one end of the scar. Later he learnt how Sister GM had announced his maiden trip to the hospital.

She had informed the students and nurses; most of them girls, that the surgeon was quite young, handsome and was married.

Many years later he would talk about these visitations with nostalgia.

On one occasion, he was due to carry out an amputation of the leg when as an afterthought, the patient called him to enquire what would happen to the part of leg that he would cut off.

The surgeon was not prepared for this question. He believed in the patient knowing all about their illness.

"There is a special place where we bury the body parts," he explained.

"In that case leave it alone," the old man requested with a measured degree of firmness.

"Why do you decline the operation?" asked the doctor, sensing alarm. "You know this is cancer and is fatal unless we amputate," the doctor explained.

"My son," the patient explained, "I do not want to be buried piecemeal. I want to be buried as one body."

No amount of persuasion would make the old man change his mind. They let him go.

***

"You can do nothing to me, I who has danced with the Queen of England!" This was the usual mantra for Odongo.

Odongo was the Municipal Engineer in the district who, when under the influence of the 'liquids of wisdom', as he called wines and spirits, would invoke the eighth wonder – that of dancing with the monarchy.

On this day, he was a patient in the ward when Salimo arrived for his routine Sunday ward round and to discharge patients. He was surprised to see his friend handcuffed to the bed and two sentries standing guard.

"Engineer, why are you here?" the doctor enquired of his friend.

This was before he noticed the redness of the eyes and swelling on the right side of Odongo's face and indeed the right side of the head.

"Moi's boys," Odongo summarised his ordeal.

This was the face of the terror years of the Moi regime. The so-called the "Twenty Years' Error".

Odongo then went on to explain how he had been picked from his house in the early hours of the previous day. He had been driven blindfolded to an unknown place where he had been tortured to silence him.

Odongo was questioning the award of tenders in the upgrading the roads in the town. The price was inflated and the winner was a shady minister in the government. The same company had done shoddy work on the previous assignment. Odongo had vowed to prevent the award on more tenders to this group.

"Salimo, this is state terror," he menacingly glared at the guards.

"Release him," the doctor ordered, "I don't examine patients in chains!"

Reluctantly the guards removed the handcuffs but warned him that if the prisoner escaped the doctor would be responsible.

At the end of the examination, he recorded all the injuries: head injury with fracture of temporal bone; urethral injury and testicular injury and soft tissue injury all over the body. He requested for X-rays of the skull, chest and the back. He also recommended exploration of the urethra under anaesthesia or 'rail-roading' as it is called, when talking of attaching wagons to the train.

"This patient requires major operation to repair his urethra," the doctor announced. Turning to the guards, he instructed, "This patient's injuries are as a result of torture or a serious vehicular accident. I want a written report on what happened."

He then went on to give further orders as follows: the prisoner was not to be chained to the hospital bed, a screen was to be put around the bed and the Station Commander was to forward a report on the patient.

"I danced with the Queen of England, these thugs in Moi's government will pay for this one day," ranted Odongo as he recovered from the anaesthesia.

"They stepped on my balls, the dogs, but I have four balls," he continued for a considerable time, till the doctor ordered mild sedation.

***

Today was a difficult day in the hospital. It was one year since Salimo had qualified. He was on his own, now a registrar. His patient was a young Somali girl, a primigravida. She was scared.

"Daktari saidia," she kept shouting every time she was gripped by a strong contraction of the uterus.

"Help me doctor, please doctor," over and over she moaned. Mariam was in labour for the first time.

Salimo was very sorry for her.

He decided to examine her and see how far she was from the birth of her baby. If birth was more than six hours away, he would administer mild sedation so she could rest and be relieved of pain.

Lying on her back with her legs in stirrups Salimo did not know what to expect when he took the sterile cotton to clean the perineum before proceeding to examine her birth canal.

Salimo was horrified to find that instead of the succulent kissing labia at the entrance of the birth canal, that are usually half hidden by the gentle bush of hair, this young mother had a smooth scar almost completely obliterating the entrance.

This was the first time Salimo had come face to face with such gross 'demolition of the goods', as he narrated to his colleagues later.

"Goods" was the term his classmate, Oburra had invented for the female sexual organ.

He had also re-named the sensual removal of the female panties a prelude to vile lovemaking 'meningectomy', comparing the usually thin and soft panties of the times that were not unlike the thin covering of the brain!

"You mean someone had meddled with the goods!" exclaimed Oburra.

Salimo found the female cut truly intriguing and abominable. He was more used to encountering the extended clitoris in the region.

"Has humanity lost motion?" Salimo wondered.

Motion is the essence of change. We move from point A to point B and experience change. Every action has an equal and opposite reaction but yet it was motion that brought true change. A shift in ideas represented motion. One person experiences motion or causes movement of ideas and feelings and society moves on. A movement in society is a collective motion of ideas, beliefs and causes of action.

How could society remain so static in matters of sexuality!

That evening, Salimo designed a thousand and one devices to replace the social function of the female cut.

One of the contraptions was based on digital exploration of the birth canal and calibration or precision re-sizing of the new gadget to restore virginity. The male thumb was identified as optimal standard.

He could, however, not decide whose thumb would be selected as the standard size of a surgically reconstructed hymen – a necessary step for patenting and preserving the digital device that Salimo had just invented.

Among the many systems of vaginal manipulation in the interest of sexuality, Salimo preferred or even glorified two.

One was the massaging of the clitoris to lengthen it.

This, he thought, served two functions. One was to control or regulate motion. Wrapped around the male organ, the ingenious organ, as he called it, it held the man and woman together in true congress until both experienced true orgasm.

Secondly, in his view it was the hallmark of the female orgasm. The long clitoris experienced erection at the time of the female orgasm and simultaneously released the grip on the male organ.

Salimo imagined that in some women the synchronised unwinding and erection at the same time could generate a force that resembled strong electric currents.

He truly marvelled at the Baganda for this sexual ingenuity.

The second sexual inventiveness that Salimo adored was the Makonde of Tanganyika. The trained and ultra-strong pelvic muscles provided the grasp.

Once the penetration occurred, the muscles literally went in a kind of friendly spasm, making sex truly blissful.

The muscles only let go once the female liaison experienced orgasm.

What Salimo did not like about the Makonde embrace though was the process of training the girls on how to lavish their men with sex.

The process was as elaborate as effective.

The novice was forced to squat above a charcoal burner while using the abdominal and pelvic muscles to swing a basket containing some grain.

To escape the scorching fire below, the young girl had to use the pelvic muscle to perform an unnatural function – that of lifting and supporting the pelvic girdle.

The tension these pelvic muscles generated was truly awesome!

Salimo loved the Baganda and the Makonde for their appreciation of human sexuality. No injury, no damage, the goods were left intact but more importantly trained to promote sexuality. To manage complex motion machines.

"Those people don't know what they are missing," John Odhiambo interjected.

He had just arrived at the tail end of the distressing discourse Salimo and Oburra were engaged in about the patient.

John had a way of grasping the gist of any discussion even if he only had heard a fraction of the tale. He proceeded to narrate his experience with a thin Somali girl.

"One day, I had a slim Somali girl for company. No sooner had we arrived in Seychelles for the weekend that she excused herself. For about thirty minutes she vanished into the bathroom to prepare herself. Having bathed she applied herbs all over, more so taking care at the profuse applications over the 'goods'! Well-marinated, the witch then had me in her; wrapped her sensuous mouth around mine together with my nose. With each of her index finger she plugged my ears and with one of her heels, she closed my rear 'exhaust' outlet."

"Gentlemen," John Odhiambo concluded with his characteristic laughter, "I only woke up 12 hours later to find the witch washed clean, taking a sip of her coffee, watching over me". John had sworn never to indulge himself in such a misadventure, "never again shall my life be endangered by a thin Somali girl!"

Through gusts of laughter, Obush, as they called Oburra, announced: "It was acute brain oedema." He then went on to inform them that during orgasm, there is acute rise in the blood pressure, sometimes twice the normal!

Salimo concluded, "All the female circumcisers should be banished to an island without women!"

He also cursed the young French doctor from MSF who on noticing the long dangling thing between the thighs of the patient on whom he had just performed a caesarean section, proceeded to chop it off!

The doctor had been in the country for only short time and had never had of the sexual technique known as *kajabale* or that Ugandan women were giving their Kenyan counterparts a run for their men!

Later he thought of 'penile angina' when he heard of another French enthusiast who, not being aware of the Makonde clutch, proceeded to engage one of them in sex. So tight was the hold on his sex organ that he thought it would be cut off and the second of the many rotations of his mate's powerful pelvis sent all his stomach contents out in one forceful explosion!

"I was going to faint both from the feint, crunch and vertigo," the student told and retold his experience.

Sex is in the mind... it is the imagination of what is hidden under the skirt... an illusion.

Motion is sensuous. Without motion all would be quiet and meaningless. There is no ailment that motion cannot treat. Stars are in continuous motion. Look at the Southern Cross and the Milky Way.

Today Salimo wants to keep going. Move in any direction as long as he is moving. The position of the sun was changing, as were the clouds. Everything beautiful is in motion. To Salimo, motion was life and all living things moved. Trees moved with the wind. Animals walked, flew and crawled. Motion unites us all. Without motion we cannot meet, love, hate or fight. The restlessness of the heart is motion.

***